# TESTIMONIALS

"Goodman and Nugent have crafted this excellent Educational Leadership book to provide a twenty-first century look at the leadership field. Well-crafted and intelligently organized, it provides advice directly from leaders; important information about critical topics such as mentoring, collaboration, strategic planning, and faculty development; and many others. As I think about courses I have taught in the past on leadership, I wish this book had been available then."

Dr. Philip A. Schmidt
CEO of inSTEMact
Past President of the TEACH-NOW Graduate School of Education

"During the years that I served in higher education, I observed many teachers who attempted the transition from the classroom to becoming a leader in education administration. Unfortunately, the ratio of those who succeeded to those who did not implies that something was missing in the transitional process. Where was the how-to manual to guide teachers through the process? *From Teacher to Leader: Paving Your Path to Education Administration answers the question.*"

Michael Maki, Ph.D.
Education Administration

"In the years I had the privilege to work with Dr. Kim Nugent, I found her to be an inspiring, tireless, and effective leader, leading with both heart and head. In this gem of a book, Drs. Goodman and Nugent not only give real-world insights and hands-on practical advice on how to make a successful transition from teacher to educational leader, but they provide a great primer for anyone desiring to transition to, improve, or enhance their leadership skills and abilities. Inspiring others to become the best version of themselves is the noble work of a good leader. This book is a hands-on guide to do just that."

Mark S. Cameron, Ph.D.
Former Higher Education Leader

"*From Teacher to Leader* provides a well-needed practical guide for people in education to make the leap from classroom to leadership. Significant sections deal with 1) insights from many who have taken this path, 2) the importance of change management and mentorship, and 3) useful self-assessments and reflective questions to prepare and launch self-development for the transition.

*From Teacher to Leader* is a grand collection of what is needed in educational leadership. It clarifies the task areas and competencies needed, has an A-Z structured pathway to navigate the shift in roles, includes insights from many who have taken this path, and the great learnings of the authors in their own transitions. Most importantly, throughout societies, the education sector has become more critical and disrupted by serious types of changes. Leadership in these organizations will be paramount!"

David W. Jamieson, Ph.D.
President, Jamieson Consulting Group, Inc, and Editor, *Organization Development Review*
Former President of the American Society of Training and Development
(ASTD, now ATD), NTL Institute for Applied Behavioral Science

"Having spent over 30 years researching the science of how to accelerate the speed of learning and behavior change, I found that the emphasis on developing critical competencies along with powerful self-reflection and the mentoring format sets this book apart from other resources. The approach of this book is a game-changer for any teacher ready to step into educational leadership."

J.W. Wilson
Executive Director, The Learning Code Institute

"Faculty members know how to write a syllabus but do they know how to write a strategic plan? They know how to mentor advisees but can they hold subordinates accountable for their performance? They are good at writing grant applications, but can they make the hard choices to balance a budget? The leap from teaching to leading requires new knowledge and skills. *From Teacher to Leader: Paving Your Path to Education Administration prepares one to make the leap*."

David Clinefelter, Ph.D.
Clinefelter Consulting, Former Education Leader as Chief Academic Officer,
Walden University and Learning House; Provost, Kaplan University;
President, Graceland University

"As an educational leader for over 40 years with advanced degrees and a plethora of experience, I can honestly say that the missing link to happiness and success as an administrator is addressed in this book. Cross-sector research on the importance of social-emotional learning and leadership, along with a window into the positive psychology movement helps us understand and balance our identity with our work to lead a wholehearted life. It is through this effort that we will encourage teachers to become educational leaders and retain quality administrators. A must read!"

Tammy Quist, ME.d. Educational Leadership
National Educational Leadership Consultant and Coach
Change Agent, Inc.

"From Teacher to Leader is a remarkable book that not only introduces the revolutionary B.A.N.K. personality system but also emphasizes the crucial role of communication and emotional intelligence in educational leadership. By embracing this powerful information, teachers-turned-leaders are equipped with the essential tools to not only communicate effectively, but also foster a nurturing environment where students are engaged in the learning process and can develop vital life skills. This book is a must-read for educators who aspire to create lasting impacts on both their teams and the students they serve."

Cheri Tree, Founder and CEO, Codebreaker Technologies.

# FROM TEACHER TO LEADER

*Paving Your Path to Education Administration*

**ERIC GOODMAN, Ph.D., and KIM NUGENT, Ed.D.**

Publisher: JETLAUNCH

ISBN: 978-1-960995-36-0 (Paperback)
ISBN: 978-1-960995-37-7 (eBook)

**Author Contact Information**

**Dr. Eric Goodman at:**
Email: eric@higheredchange.com
Website: www.higheredchange.com

**Dr. Kim Nugent at:**
Email: Kim@drnugentspeaks.com
Website: www.drnugentspeaks.com

# TABLE OF CONTENTS

# INTRODUCTION TO ACADEMIC LEADERSHIP

So, what does it really take to transition from being a teacher to a leader? Our why.

## Eric's Story

When I was growing up, I wanted to be a doctor so I could help people. However, once in college, I realized I loved the world of business and didn't want to spend so much time in school. So, after a few years, I changed my major to business. I thought I was done with my formal education, but my parents instilled in me a love of learning and a curiosity about the world. My father grew up in the projects on the south side of Chicago and never went to college. However, he was always learning skills to advance in his career. So, it wasn't long before I pursued my master's degree while working. I had an inspiring professor, R. Wayne Boss, who saw in me something I hadn't seen in myself, and he encouraged me to pursue my doctorate.

After leaving the corporate world and earning my Ph.D. from the University of Colorado at Boulder in Business Administration, I fell in love with teaching. While the program prepared me for the world of research, with the support of my amazing wife, Kelley, I pursued a faculty role at a teaching-focused state university rather than a tier-1 research university. In the spirit of lifelong learning, I immersed myself in learning how to be as effective as possible in the classroom. I was fortunate to take part in one of a handful of Ph.D. programs in the nation at the time that required extensive training (well over 100 hours) in the art and science of teaching, from how to write a syllabus, hold office hours, use the Socratic method, to being observed and videotaped teaching and critiqued and mentored along the way. After graduating and in my new faculty role, I found that while many of my peers had the specific discipline knowledge from their field of study, they didn't have the expertise related to how to teach.

I quickly added value to the university-wide faculty development committee and received university-wide recognition for teaching in my first year. I remember reading Parker Palmer's *The Courage to Teach*, which was hot off the press, and his view that "good teaching requires self-knowledge, integrity, and community." He also talked about our developing identity. It was only later that I realized how these ideas were related to the concept of emotional intelligence. Also, having taught many business courses like management and leadership concepts, I recognized he touched on many leadership theories (e.g., servant leadership, trait leadership, transformational leadership, etc.).

However, when I became a dean at 30, I found that there weren't the same training opportunities or the type of support and community of peers to learn from at my new university. I was fortunate that I had already studied business extensively and had the experience of managing dozens of employees in the corporate world. I quickly discovered that many others didn't have that same type of management experience and that there were a few books, albeit limited in scope, to prepare me for the complexities of being a leader in academia.

In reflecting on my transition from teacher to leader and the lessons I've learned from over a decade as a business school dean, along with many years as a VP of Education/ Chief Academic Officer, I recognize a theme in my career has been my ability to earn the trust of others and manage change. This has been a critical element in influencing others in many complex, fast-moving higher education systems. When I think about the experiences I've had in helping several colleges move to university status by introducing master's degree programs, navigating the complexity of multi-state, multi-campus institutions, launching online universities, leading the nation's largest competency-based college of business, improving student retention, and launching online programs to help colleges survive COVID-19, all while improving the student experience and outcomes, none of those things could have been accomplished without trust!

One concept I learned even before I was a teacher is from Stephen Covey's *The 7 Habits of Highly Effective People*, namely the concept of the "Emotional Bank Account." This is a metaphorical account that represents the level of trust and goodwill that exists between two people. It is in that spirit that this book should help pave the path for you, from teacher to leader, with the key competencies to be successful. While I specify a few competencies in this book, they are certainly not intended to be mutually exclusive of the competencies that will lead to trust. Rather, you'll find that the entire book includes critical ideas and competencies that will lead you to a successful transition as a leader—and you can bank on that!

Just as with a financial bank account, we can make deposits and withdrawals from our Emotional Bank Account with others. Covey suggests we build trust with others by making consistent deposits in the Emotional Bank Account. Deposits can come in many forms, such as showing kindness and consideration, being honest and transparent, and following through on commitments. Each deposit we make builds up a reserve of trust, which makes it easier to weather the occasional withdrawals that may occur in any relationship.

In contrast, when we make withdrawals from the Emotional Bank Account, we damage the trust and goodwill that exists between us and the other person. Withdrawals can occur when we break commitments, behave in ways that are disrespectful or hurtful, or cannot show empathy or understanding. These withdrawals can quickly erode the trust that we have built up and can damage the relationship.

Covey's theory of the Emotional Bank Account suggests that building strong relationships requires a consistent effort to make deposits and avoid withdrawals. By doing so, we can create a foundation of trust and goodwill that enables us to work effectively with others, even in challenging situations. Trust is a critical component of any successful workplace. It forms the foundation for teams to collaborate, get along, and achieve success. Building trust in the workplace is essential for retaining valuable employees, fostering collaboration and innovation, and ultimately creating a more productive, engaged workforce.

As you journey from teacher to leader, it is also important to mention the "Law of the Lid," a concept introduced by John Maxwell. The law states that the effectiveness of a leader is limited by their level of personal development. The lid represents the ceiling of a leader's potential, and this lid can only be lifted by increasing the leader's ability, knowledge, and character. If a leader wants to maximize their impact, they must continuously work on their personal growth and development. If that is you, then you're in the right place. My why in life and in writing this book is to help empower you to discover, leverage, and maximize your potential so that you become the best version of yourself. As an educator, you can affect the lives of others, and as Nelson Mandela suggests, "Education is the most powerful weapon which you can use to change the world." My vision is to create a community of confident leaders who I inspire to embrace their unique gifts so that together we can positively affect the world. I'm committed to helping share best practices and proven systems to help speed up your success. After all, there is no need to reinvent the wheel. Success leaves clues. As you read this book, you'll find the steppingstones on your transition to being a powerful leader in education, where you can create a culture of trust and reap the rewards of having greater influence and impact on countless lives. Enjoy the journey!!

## Kim's Story

You might wonder what my why in writing the book might be. While I had held many administrative roles in the hospitality industry, I wanted to transition into higher education and become a faculty member because of one of my professors when I was an undergraduate at the University of Houston at Hilton College. His name was Dr. Raymond Goodman. He made it look so easy. I earned my MBA at the University of St. Thomas. My first position in higher education was as an adjunct faculty member at the University of Houston. I took courses such as the Dale Carnegie Public Speaking course, hired a speech coach, joined professional organizations, and, each year, took continuing education classes to develop myself. Teaching at Hilton College was an honor.

During my hospitality career at Hilton Hotels, Inc., I earned my doctorate degree in Curriculum and Instruction from the University of Houston. While I was working in the hospitality industry and teaching part time, it was not enough. I wanted to fully transition into a full-time teaching position. Eventually, after I earned my doctorate, I could leave the University of Houston and secure a full-time teaching position.

I truly believed it was a perfect fit, and I had found my dream job. I loved the students. I loved thinking of creative ways to introduce new concepts and seeing the light bulbs go on from each of them. I loved the questions and the ways they inspired me to think differently.

I was totally committed to learning my new profession every day and becoming the best faculty member. I went back to school and earned a master's degree in Instructional Design and Online Learning.

All was going well until the dean came to me and asked if I had ever thought about becoming a dean. Frankly, the answer was no. He said I should think about it, and think about it I did. I could not imagine leaving the classroom. So, the dean came back a few days later and said, "I know you love teaching, and you are affecting students' lives. Over the course of a quarter, it is probably 125 students, which is great. Being an administrator, you can affect thousands of lives as a dean." So, I thought about it and applied for the dean's position and was hired.

This is not a typical career track. I had never been a program director, registrar, or career services administrator. The dean expedited the promotion, as he was being promoted to the corporate office for a more senior role, and there was some urgency. The dean sent me to a training session on the software application the school was using for the registrar function a week prior to my starting in the role. When I returned from the trip, I learned my brother Geff had committed suicide. When I shared the information with the dean, he asked if I needed time off; I declined, stating that work would be best. I was so wrong.

Looking back at it, I should have taken the time off to deal with my grief. Self-care should always come first, but when you are in education, you take care of others first. I have learned this lesson the hard way. This was one of the most painful losses in my life, and the result is I look at life so differently and know tomorrow is not promised. I now live each day to the fullest. I look at people with a new sense of curiosity and empathy.

I started the new role the following Tuesday. It was so hard. It was harder than any administrative role I had ever had before in the hospitality industry. I had never used the registrar software system and had not been a program chair. There was internal strife on the education team, and retention was down. It was time for the semiannual program advisory meetings to be held, and we were going through an accreditation visit. I made a lot of mistakes along the way and would not have been successful if not for the grace of the program chairs and especially our culinary director. I wish there had been a book like this for me.

Finally, I found my way and found joy in all my new accountabilities. What I learned for myself was I had to be me. I taught a class once a year and continued to help faculty become their best selves through a commitment to ongoing faculty development. I supported program chairs in understanding policies and helping with innovative retention strategies, just to name a few of the rewards. The best experience each year was the new student orientation and graduation ceremonies, which we held several times a year. They totally inspired me when they entered our school, so eager to change their lives and begin a new profession. Each graduation, when "Pomp and Circumstance" started playing, looking out to see the graduates always brought tears to my eyes. I know what it took for each student to cross the finish line, and that was never lost on me.

As my experience and skills developed, I eventually became a campus president. I have been honored to work with some of the best higher education professionals, of which many remain friends today. Each of them grew in their administrative abilities, and many became campus presidents as well. I hope my legacy will demonstrate I helped people become their very best.

Another beautiful thing is I met many great professionals along the journey. We often found we were dealing with the same issues and, together, found innovative solutions to solve complex situations by simply sharing.

During my educational career journey, I met Dr. Eric Goodman about twelve years ago. While we never worked directly together, we would reach out every few years. Our latest touch-base call resulted in the idea of collaboration in writing a book to help teachers who are considering an administrative role in support and mentorship. We know you cannot get there on your own. We certainly hope you find this book practical. I know I wish I had a book to help me so many years ago.

So, you think you want to be a leader... What is your why? Your purpose?

_____

_____

_____

_____

_____

_____

_____

_____

_____

_____

_____

_____

_____

_____

_____

_____

_____

_____

_____

_____

_____

# ADVICE FROM LEADERS

**If someone is considering becoming a higher education administrator, what are some pitfalls to be aware of?**

- There are three that come to mind for new leaders to consider. First, recognize and embrace that your core skills—in this case, as a teacher—are no longer vital to success. When running the show, you need a solid set of leadership skills, which may have nothing to do with your teaching skills. Second, since you are new to leadership, your staff, peers, and the board will most likely challenge you. Have a plan for what to do when challenged. Third, be aware you will be constantly watched, assessed, and evaluated. You are now held to a higher standard than in previous jobs.

- Unwillingness to shed legacy systems of serving students.

- The importance of the Ph.D. for credibility and opportunity for advancement. Experience is not enough. An understanding of what motivates faculty.

- This is based on secondary education administration. They should ask themselves why they want to enter administration. If it's just to get out of the classroom or to work more individually and less with others, the jump may fall far below expectations. Each level of leadership calls for a variety of styles and abilities. Just because someone is a good assistant principal doesn't mean they have what is needed to be a solid principal. The challenges are so different.

- The journey to administration is very long and not open to giving opportunities to those who don't have the experience to start. It also takes a long time to move up to management. Compensation is low, and it is not rewarding. The other challenge is that changing the industry is not easy at all.

- Personnel issues can get tricky, legal issues can arise, and working long hours at times; it's a great deal of responsibility.

- You don't control your day, so many other items pop up that warrant solving...but a lot of nonsense. It's a transition from being great in the classroom to being great with others that you can't easily reward or pressure.

- Making promises to their teacher friends. They forget it is business and not personal.

- Time considerations are a major factor. Being an administrator requires a flexible work schedule and the ability to adapt to the constant change in any higher education workplace.

- There are a variety of pressures. Some come from the structure and rigidity of higher education. Some arise from the limited resources that most institutions face. Some are due to political pressures from both the right and left.

- Depending on the role one takes on, you may find yourself in a referee role rather than a leadership role. As an education administrator, you serve many constituents—students, faculty, unions, superiors, politicians, parents, and other institutions. The successful administrator must understand the need to work with these many constituents. Higher education currently faces significant enrollment challenges due to changing demographics, shifts during COVID, and competition. Education administrators must address these challenges.

- In higher education, very few faculty understand the business of higher education. Without enrollment growth, institutions must cut budgets. Faculty dislike seeing budgets and programs cut; it is a difficult transition. Likewise, the highly unionized higher education environment presents challenges that very few faculty are prepared to address.

- The loss of your identity as a researcher is inevitable. It will take a back seat. You will have a different relationship with colleagues as a line manager, and you often become a generalist rather than a subject specialist.

- If you are internally promoted, it changes your relationships with colleagues. Our research on the AACC competencies shows that faculty are often unaware of budget processes and institutional policies and procedures. This is true disproportionately for people of color and women.

- Absolute clarity about the right choice is rare. Avoid the temptations of analysis paralysis. There comes a time when consulting with more stakeholders is no longer warranted. And you will not please everyone.

- The politics. You need to learn how to navigate politics. And I define politics as "the way things get done." Power and influence come from many positions, not only those at the top. Also, most administrators tend to solve administrators' problems with administrators' solutions. These are not necessarily the same problems students or faculty have. Both students' and faculty's problems are more important than administrators' problems. But they rarely get the same time, attention, and resources. Additionally, administrators' solutions can create more problems for students and faculty.

- Very political in some institutions. I worked for a school that had no room for advancement, even if you had a doctorate and experience. I spent nine years in the same position. I applied for many jobs but never even got an interview. If they did not know you or you were not liked, you did not go anywhere.

**Based on your experience, what are some reasons teachers are unsuccessful in transitioning into education administration?**

- There is often no formal training or succession planning. Much like higher education faculty are often not trained as educators but subject matter experts, faculty who are transitioning to leadership often have no formal training. Programs through ACE, AACC, AAC&U, and other organizations can be helpful in the transition.

- They do not really understand administration. Their mindsets never seem to move out of the teaching mode. You must understand systems, follow policies and procedures, and be consistent with practices. Decisions must follow the policies and procedures rather than on a case-by-case basis. If you do for one student, you must do for all, or you set the school up for lawsuits.

- Three come to mind. Number one is relying on technical skills for success in the new role. The technical skills developed an experience base and generated certain individual successes and accomplishments that contributed to your being chosen as a leader. However, leaders use this experience to develop and empower teams and delegate the performance of most technical things to achieve a higher-level mission. So, you may have once achieved great satisfaction by seeing students in your class "get it" and succeed due to your teaching prowess, but you now must find a way for all your teaching staff to achieve those results. You can't teach their classes for them, so by empowering them via training, support, motivation, shared experiences, *feedback*, curriculum, and more, the entire organization can achieve as well as you once did technically. Number two is communication. Perhaps a leader's greatest responsibility is to clearly chart the course and communicate expectations, followed by more communication about progress. Your team(s) can't get enough communication from you. Number three is recognizing that you must give feedback after setting expectations for your teams. Some people shy away from giving feedback; they view it as confrontation. But it is derelict for a leader not to clearly set expectations and then reinforce the expectations with clear feedback and related dialogue. If the staff does not know where they stand, how can they possibly know how to improve? If they don't improve, how will the organization achieve greatness?

- It is difficult to encourage teachers to get into secondary administration. Many people look at the incredibly long hours, politics, and school district gobbledygook administrators deal with and want no part of it. I've seen outreach programs to help identify and court potential future school leaders to make the change work by letting them learn from sitting administrators and shadowing where possible.

- They lack the skill set necessary to be successful.

- Teaching can include a performance aspect that administration rarely offers. If you're going to miss commanding attention from the front of a classroom, look for other ways to experience something similar.

- We find that many faculty members lack supervisory experience or significant leadership experience.

- As a former teacher, I had to learn how to manage up as well as down. I was better at managing employees reporting to me (more like dealing with students) than managing up. I had to learn to communicate and promote our work to those who oversaw our work. In general, teachers have a lot of autonomy in the classroom, and as administrators, they focus on the classroom and the quality of what goes on there. However, there are also significant institutional goals that may clash with the ideal for the classroom.

- They still think like a teacher and are not strategic.

- They do not want to make hard decisions that affect colleagues, who they still view as peers. There is inadequate training and development.

- Time management and the need to develop long hours for leadership jobs surprise some new leaders. Others are poor at communication—both with those they lead and those they report to.

- Teaching is a different skill set from administration. Many can't make the transition. Whereas you can change class content on the fly and implement it, that does not happen at the administrative level most of the time. For some individuals, taking responsibility for the failures of others who do not plan, refuse to take ownership, or fail to treat their responsibilities with the necessary seriousness is difficult. Leadership can be lonely. It is difficult to share your issues with a large number of people.

- You need to make tough decisions when it comes to scheduling faculty, training faculty, and managing them. You need to connect with them but cannot let them be in charge of your everyday decisions.

**What do you consider to be the most important qualities of a successful leader in education?**

- Empathy... Understanding what a teacher goes through and your role in helping with that process. This doesn't mean tolerance for inferior performance, but understanding the challenges. Then make the challenges diminish so they can do a better job.

- Humility and a genuine interest in human development.

- The ability to communicate effectively with all levels within the institution.

- Be a good listener and be of service to everyone.

- Personal and professional integrity. Compassionate about people and mission.

- Curiosity, humility, trust, integrity, accountability, and valuing the organization's success over personal advancement.

- Successful leaders can motivate their teams, move them forward, and explain necessary changes in terms of new learning techniques and platforms so that those changes are embraced and adopted.
- Honesty and integrity, good sense of self, genuinely enjoy students and staff/faculty.
- Leadership, strategic thinking, planning, and listening.
- A sense of purpose and the ability to communicate that in a manner that brings people with you.

**How will workplace trends impact the knowledge, skills, and attitudes needed by people working in higher education today and in the future?**

- The first two require flexibility and the ability to nimbly change without awakening the sleeping bureaucracy. The latter may instill a deeper commitment to ethics and personal truth. I think it will be more difficult to identify non-original work in the future, especially as AI technology is readily accessible.
- Education administrators must understand the relationship between enrollments, budgets, and success. They must be prepared to make difficult enrollment and program decisions.
- Beginning or continuing your personal equity and inclusion journey is a must. This is hard, deeply personal work, but it must be done if you want to work in higher education. Take risks and cultivate creative problem-solving strategies or listen to and promote those who do. Fast, flexible strategies will be needed to adapt to the rapidly changing circumstances that are here and still coming.
- Be aware of trends locally and globally.
- Digital skills and an entrepreneurial mindset must be balanced with discipline-specific knowledge.
- Flexibility rather than specific degrees has always been more important than the public realizes; an appreciation for a broad general education is going to grow again.
- In terms of online programs, this will impact traditional brick-and-mortar schools. People will no longer be needed on campuses. The days of going to campus will eventually be obsolete. Traditional schools may not exist in the future. Technology is going to "dumb" things down. Students will not learn how to do things the old way. This will lead to students not knowing how to interact with each other. Social skills will not be well developed—a major concern for future employment and success. Instructors face evaluations, which can be detrimental to their careers if they don't just pass students. Holding students accountable for their learning is needed. It takes one bad review or complaint to make students happy for not doing the work. Instructors often must compromise their integrity because schools want problems to go away instead of holding the student accountable for not doing the work outlined in the syllabus.

- The bureaucracy of higher education may make it obsolete in preparing its students for life after college.

- Flexibility and openness to new ideas and approaches.

- Constant learning will be even more important. This can be a challenge for more mature people.

- There needs to be just-in-time education. Stackable skills and easily transferred skills.

- If we don't accept the fact that change is inevitable and don't get in front of it, the country will keep losing its competitiveness in workforce development and research.

- Those leading higher education will have many more challenges and shorter time frames to act.

- Leaders need to be prepared to face the above issues with creativity, knowledge, and, at times, swift response.

**What gaps do you see in the training and education of your organization's employees working in education administration?**

- We're not deliberate enough about teaching people to work in teams.

- How to be agents of change, identify potential roadblocks, and make a plan for the future.

- Ha-ha—what training? Most of the higher education administrators I know did not receive formal training in the business of higher education. Clearly, enrollment management, budget management, and personnel management are all skills that successful administrators need to develop.

- Lack of formal training in leadership and succession planning.

- There are no real training and development programs. Everything's done online. Staff train themselves. There are no actual orientations. Employees are just told to go online to do orientation. Just because technology makes things convenient does not mean people learn what they need to learn.

- How to have difficult conversations and manage underperformance.

- Staying in touch with the developing needs of the incoming and existing student body.

- More seminars and other organized events for administrators from different colleges and universities in attendance. Experts in the top trends present their area of focus, followed by discussion groups from a mix of institutions discussing how to integrate these trends into current practices.

- Lack of experience in other organizations. People get stuck with one way of knowing, doing, and being. Also, lack of seeing that personal goal achievement should not come at the expense of organizational goal achievement. Using data in a continuous improvement cycle is paramount. Many do not have this skill and are afraid to learn.

They fear measurement will be a "gotcha" moment, and lack of results implies a lack of personal worth and commitment. Planning—mostly operational planning. There is a general lack of being able to set goals and then create a plan to get there, utilizing data to both set the goals and inform the strategy.

- There is not much in the way of training!
- The training is not up to date and not practical in actual settings.
- Technology and its relevance to the marketplace. The transition from a traditional four-year experience to a new method of teaching and degree conveyance. Certificates will grow in importance.
- Most people who become department chairs have little to no previous training as leaders or with administrative responsibilities.
- My organization has been at the forefront of virtual education and training employees at all levels, including administrators, to use virtual tools to succeed.
- Training, training, training. Keeping up with hiring practices, enrollment trends, recruitment of adjuncts, and ensuring new administration understands legal implications.

**What skills or knowledge do great administrators possess?**

- Listening skills; systemic thinking—I see so many falter considering only the information presented rather than looking for what's not in front of them.
- Empathy, creativity, analytics, openness, and strategic thinking.
- Leadership, influencing, and negotiation skills.
- Emotional intelligence, leadership skills, and enrollment management skills.
- Strategic thinking and implementation of knowledge. Ability to inspire others. A true understanding of data and information.
- Communicating across multiple constituent groups. Integrity. Time and stress management skills. Understanding the uniqueness of higher education organizations as businesses and services.
- Data literacy, continuous improvement, goal setting, planning, team building.
- They build and maintain trust. They communicate effectively and move the organization forward.
- Integrity, strong communication skills, a vision for the future.
- They understand that if they have anyone, they lead first before attempting to lead anyone anywhere.
- They can work with different groups of people within their organization to lead and manage change. They have people skills, including the ability to read other people and see what motivates them to help the team connect and produce valuable results.

- Great written and oral communication skills, integrity in leadership, motivational and collaborative skills, empathy, and fairness.
- Discipline, fairness, and equality. Gratitude, resource acquisition, innovation, vision, and fiscal expertise.
- The ability to listen and change their minds.
- Communication, teamwork, leadership characteristics.
- Good listener, flexibility, ability to multitask, and must enjoy working with people.

## What advice would you give teachers who desire to become education leaders?

- Find a great mentor!
- Think carefully about your priorities and your reasons for doing so; more money isn't a good enough reason.
- Get into it for the right reasons.
- Your classroom experience is an important asset, but there are cases where administrative requirements will clash with principles you hold dear from that experience, and the best decision isn't always going to be clearly indexed to that experience.
- Really think about what the job entails. Not everyone will be good at administration. Your focus will no longer be teaching and research. It becomes about managing people; if you are not good at working with people, then administration is not for you.
- Learn the business of higher education. Get an MBA, and it will help you succeed.
- Join different groups in your educational workplace to find out what is happening in different areas of your college or university. Look for a position that might interest you as an administrator that would also involve teaching, should you choose to return to the classroom (or stay in it). You have valuable knowledge as an educator. Find ways to share that effectively.
- Get a Ph.D., and take courses/get experience in project management, budgeting, and influencing and negotiating.
- Teachers would transition to faculty by adjunct when they can. The other possibility would be to get on the student services track by starting as an advisor.
- Think carefully about making the transition. The priorities are different, and there is less freedom to act alone. Everything is done in collaboration or consultation with others. But remember, you have a perspective from teaching that others probably don't. You can help keep them focused on what matters in higher education.
- Read, take part in workshops when available, and learn from mentors.
- Being a leader isn't about you. It is about building a happy, productive team that makes a difference.

- Gain committee and project experience, take on leadership roles within, step up and volunteer when asked, show up at college events, be a leader within faculty groups, and chair important committees if possible.
- Rewards are different from what they have known.

**What strategies have you found successful in your career journey?**

- Get formal training. Find a mentor. Do research on your own.
- Respect for other people's opinions and experiences. Networking and building relationships. Watching and learning from mentors. Openness and honesty.
- Help others along the way, identify new talent, and mentor individuals to get them where they want to be. Say yes when asked to take on more or different responsibilities.
- Embrace change. If you aren't changing, you are static, and standing still means you might get hit by a car.
- Stick to your integrity. You may lose your job, but not your career. Refocus on the priorities when you feel overwhelmed by too many of them. See something, say something. You can make the organization a better place by not ignoring problems. Stay flexible. Priorities shift, strategies bust. Be ready to try a new approach if the original one isn't working.
- Being open and accepting change is the most important aspect of working in administration. Be open to the ideas of others, and don't be a micromanager to all employees. Some people need autonomy, and others need to be micromanaged.
- Understanding what is most important to my superiors. Willingness to upset the apple cart. Looking at how other institutions do things.
- Questioning authority and conventional ways of doing business.
- I have moved from classroom to classroom, college to university, and position to position seamlessly. There has always been a new challenge for me in terms of where I was teaching and what or how I was using the course material. I have always embraced change and moved from teaching or working in person to teaching and working online. Embracing challenges has been my mantra.
- Wait to announce a decision until I have vetted it through many others. Listen more than talk. Learn who the naysayers are and work with them on anything pressing.
- Learning to understand and align with institutional goals and objectives. Influencing and negotiating skills. Networking.
- Enrollment administration. There seems to be a lack of planning and execution on these plans in this role.
- Making myself available to faculty. Seeking faculty thoughts and their pulse. Communicating constantly.

- Be willing to move. Remain current in your expertise area. Read materials pertaining to higher education leadership.
- Development of a great team to get the work done quickly and efficiently. Work to develop a cohesive team.
- A learning mindset: the ability to put the benefits of the school before any single individual.

**Which jobs in education administration are the most difficult to recruit qualified employees?**

- Again, it depends on discipline and is different between universities and community colleges because of pay rates. Also, pressures for hiring minorities aren't helping. For community colleges, we have challenges at all levels, from the department chair to the instruction side. The student services are easier, but administrative services like the business office and facilities are more difficult.
- Department chairs.
- Front-line administrators are the most difficult to train and recruit, including those who work directly with faculty and then report to higher administrators.
- For us right now—adjunct faculty and qualified library practitioners.
- CEI officers, CFO, and CEO.
- There's no easy recruitment path. It's often a call by the people who wish to do the job.
- Middle management (e.g., subject or department).
- Financial!
- My experience suggests finding a qualified team in the provost's office is the hardest.

Contributors to the advice section include Jane Allen, Dr. Shah Ardalan, Mark Bannister, Cheryl Boncoure, Jonathan Burdick, Russell Jay Frohardt, Katy Hill, Tim Jeffcoat, Rose Kolby, Joe Kolenda, Kathy Lamos, Dr. Diane McGeehan, Dr. Mary McRae, Robert Peterson, Dawn Samson and Steven Tello.

Reflection Question: Based on the advice, what are your takeaways?

_____

_____

_____

_____

_____

# THE NUTS-AND-BOLTS: SURVEY DATA-COMPETENCIES TO BE AN EDUCATIONAL LEADER

We surveyed education leaders across the United States to determine the critical skills one must develop in one's career (January 2023). The sooner you master these skills, the more confident you will become and the more satisfied you will be in your administrative role.

They are budgeting and financial management, change management, collaboration, communication, conflict resolution, decision-making, ethics, faculty development, influence, innovation and creativity, leadership styles, lifelong learning, organizational strategies, project management, strategic planning, teamwork, and time management skills.

## Budgeting and Financial Management

As an educational leader, it is crucial to have a solid comprehension of budgeting and financial management to successfully manage an organization's financial resources. This is especially true as schools grapple with the new realities and aftershocks of the COVID-19 pandemic and changing demographics. It is essential for schools to have a good understanding of their financials to make informed decisions and ensure their long-term financial stability. To effectively oversee a school's finances, certain abilities and knowledge need to be attained and polished. Understanding financial operations is the foremost of these. This involves knowledge of the budgeting procedure, allocation of income and costs, and methods to augment revenue and diminish expenditures.

Leaders must be able to evaluate, interpret, and use financial data in their daily decisions. Developing financial acumen is a critical area and a typical gap for a teacher promoted into a leadership role. As a leader, one needs to understand how the school is doing regarding its financial health to make informed decisions on the resources and when and when not to spend. While some people may have a foundation in financial data, it is important to grasp cash flow, accounting principles and practices, and the financial statements used to show an organization's financial health. Leaders should develop the skills to interpret financial data, including reading and understanding balance sheets, income statements, and cash flow statements. Knowing how to analyze financial information and make decisions based on the analysis is essential for any educational leader. Financial metrics, such as net tuition revenues, operating expenses, and research grants, provide insight into the financial performance of a school. Areas such as net tuition revenues measure the number of tuition dollars received minus any discounts or scholarships provided. Operating expenses measure the money spent on day-to-day operations, such as salaries and supplies. Research grants measure the external funding generated from grants and contracts, which help to fund research initiatives and other university services. Finally, leaders should be able to evaluate a school's financial health by assessing financial trends, executing financial audits, and using financial models.

It is important to recognize that a school's financial health is typically determined by analyzing a combination of operational and financial metrics. Operational metrics, such as student enrollment, graduation rates, and student-faculty ratios, offer insight into the effectiveness of the school's recruitment efforts, the quality of its academic offerings, and the overall health of the institution. By analyzing operational and financial metrics, schools can better understand their overall performance and ability to successfully recruit and retain students.

**What are the key budgeting principles for a school?**

Considering budget constraints, it is vital to understand the fundamentals of budgeting and financial planning. Budgeting is a crucial part of financial management, and it is necessary to distribute resources responsibly and appropriately. Here are key budgeting principles to consider when planning and maintaining a budget:

1. *Understand the financial context.* Recognize that broader forces at work are shaped by macroeconomic conditions, industry, competitors, government, regulation, and other factors like demographics. In the past few years, there have been significant financial pressures, given the effects of COVID on student enrollment and persistence. Fortunately, there was government aid to assist schools in this situation. The more you understand the broader environment, the more likely you will make an informed decision. While many schools are nonprofit, regardless of the status, there are financial needs and cash flow realities to keep the lights on, so to speak, as you serve students. In some settings, financial metrics and goals may be used to measure performance, whether it is a growth or profitability target or sometimes identifying necessary cost reductions, which we have seen a fair amount of, especially in K-12 systems.

2. *Prioritize requirements.* It is important to prioritize requirements and allocate assets accordingly. This involves ensuring that resources are directed to the most essential areas, such as student and faculty support, research, and infrastructure. Keep in mind that, based on the school's mission, these priorities may differ. As a leader, it is important that you make financial decisions that support the institution's long-term viability.

3. *Formulate a balanced budget.* Some organizations set financial goals from the top, whereas others do so from the bottom or perhaps a hybrid combination. Ideally, this is a process where the goals are linked to the organizational strategy. Remember, a

budget represents the school's commitment of resources to your work and a set of boundaries for your actions. After all, you can't spend money that you don't have! It is important to understand how the budget is set as a new leader and the details of how goals are set, how to gather information to determine the feasibility of the goals, and how best to provide input in the event you encounter an unreasonable financial goal. Remember, you may encounter a boss who doesn't understand the day-to-day operational realities of your area, so it is your job to inform and influence your boss as much as possible for the good of the organization. After all, a balanced budget should be created that considers both revenue sources and expenses. This will guarantee that the budget can meet the demands of the school and that it does not become over- or under-subscribed.

4. *Plan for the future.* Budgeting should consider the future needs of the college or university. This may include investing in new technology, expanding programs, and creating new initiatives. As a leader, understanding the school's business model will allow you to identify levers you may use to improve performance. It will also help you recognize where constraints may limit your ability or choices in the future.

5. *Track performance.* Performance should be tracked and monitored to ensure that the budget is meeting its objectives and that any changes are being made in a timely manner. Most times, you're likely to inherit existing formats for measuring financial performance. You must focus on reviewing this information promptly to make better decisions. Keep in mind that there may be unforeseen events that affect your school. For example, no one was expecting the far-reaching implications of COVID, so it is important to question your operating assumptions and periodically review and update them as necessary, which can help ensure that resources are being used effectively and efficiently.

By following these key budgeting principles, a leader can make responsible financial decisions while meeting their financial goals. These principles can also help ensure that the school remains financially sustainable in the long term.

## What are the types of budgets?

In the education sector, financial planning is critical to the success of any institution. Two types of budgets that play a pivotal role in ensuring smooth operations are the operating and capital budgets. An operating budget is a comprehensive financial plan that outlines the day-to-day expenses and revenue of the institution. It covers essential expenses like salaries, benefits, utilities, maintenance, and supplies. Typically created annually, the operating budget sustains the ongoing expenses of the institution.

In contrast, a capital budget is a financial plan that outlines the long-term investment in fixed assets such as buildings, equipment, and infrastructure. Unlike an operating budget, a capital budget is created for a more extended period, usually three to five years, and funds larger projects and initiatives. The primary difference between the two budgets is their purpose. The operating budget funds the routine operations of the institution, while the capital budget funds long-term investments that will have a lasting impact on the institution. In summary, both budgets are crucial to the success of any educational institution, and an effective financial plan should include both.

In any institution, it is important to connect with functional area leaders involved more closely with financial oversight to use their experience. Having the ability to learn from the chief financial officer, along with other individuals in accounting, is critical to your success. Be sure to contact them for help and explore some resources below if you'd like to learn more.

## Resources

**Book:** Brigham, E.F & Ehrhardt, M.C. (2016). Financial Management: Theory & Practice. Cengage Learning.

**Book:** Shim, J. K., & Siegel, J. G. (2011). Budgeting Basics and Beyond. John Wiley & Sons.

Finance: "What Managers Need to Know from Harvard Business Review"
https://www.youtube.com/watch?v=aJsmJsd6GIw

Access the wide range of videos available on various financial and budgeting topics available on this YouTube channel:
https://www.youtube.com/@CorporateFinanceAcademy

## Reflection Questions

1. What areas of budgeting and financial management do I need to develop a deeper understanding of?

   _____

   _____

   _____

   _____

   _____

2. How can I effectively manage the budgeting process, including developing a budget, tracking expenses, and adjusting the budget as needed?

   _____

   _____

   _____

   _____

   _____

3. How can we ensure we align budget decisions with the strategic goals and priorities of my institution?

   _____

   _____

   _____

   _____

   _____

## Change Management

Change is constant; this is one of the more challenging things for people to accept. This is true even when there is an obvious need for change, so academic leaders must understand the concept of change management to successfully lead their institutions. Change management focuses on the capability of effectively planning, implementing, and controlling adjustments that take place within an organization. It requires a comprehensive procedure that involves analyzing the current situation, establishing the desired outcome, and constructing and using strategies to accomplish this goal. This is especially pertinent for academic leaders, who guide their schools through different stages of advancement and development. An academic leader must evaluate the present situation, devise a strategy to reach the desired end, and then manage the execution of the plan. Change management enables an academic leader to detect and handle potential hazards, as well as recognize and capitalize on potential opportunities. To effectively manage change, an academic leader must have a precise understanding of how people will likely react to change along with the process.

First, it is helpful for you to think about how accepting you are of change and whether you embrace most changes or find yourself concerned about losing the status quo. Do you typically embrace change or fight it? Of course, if it's a change you want, then it may be easy. However, if you don't want a change, frustration, anger, and resistance often occur. The same is true for other people and how they react to change. There will be times when your ability to embrace change and lead the way will be critical as a leader. You can become skilled at adapting to change and then model how others will accept and implement change. It is important to distinguish between situational changes, which occur more quickly and abruptly, such as a new job or process, and other types of change. With any change, there is a corresponding transition, which is the process of change, including the psychological aspects people go through to come to terms with a new situation.

I remember when I first made the professional transition from being a teacher to an education leader; it was a challenge I had to face head-on. Foremost, I believe that effective change management begins with understanding the reasons change is necessary and desired. In my case, I recognized an opportunity based on my skill set to stretch myself and pursue a leadership role where I could have a greater impact on the university and other faculty/students. Change management is a process and set of tools used to help organizations transition from their current state to their desired future state. It is a systematic approach to managing the people side of change and ensuring the successful implementation of new initiatives, policies, and processes.

With any major change in a professional setting, it's important to understand how to manage the transition effectively. Force field analysis, developed by Kurt Lewin (1951), is a great tool to use in such situations. Force field analysis is simply a tool to identify the forces supporting and opposing the change. In some ways, this notion builds on Newton's third law of motion, namely that forces always act in equal but opposite pairs. For every action, there is an equal and opposite reaction. So, if you push on something, it will push back with a force equal in strength to the force you exerted. To shift the balance, you have to determine how to reduce the forces opposing the change and perhaps strengthen the forces supporting the change while identifying the key stakeholders that need to be engaged in the change process.

Lewin (1947) is widely considered the father of change management. His simple change model reflects a three-step process that helps identify the need for change, plan out the change process, and implement the change. This approach focuses on best managing the transition from one state to another. It comprises three major steps:

1. Unfreezing the current state
2. Moving to the new state
3. Refreezing the new state

Some people also talk about a fourth step where you evaluate the changes.

A similar model to Lewin's was proposed by William Bridges (1980), and while he focuses on the psychosocial aspects of organizational change, the notion is similar. This model builds on Lewin's transition process and helps employees understand the emotional aspects of change. Bridges suggests the following stages:

1. Endings: People are letting go of the past, able to see something end, and may experience loss or grief as they recognize what is different.
2. Neutral zone: People navigate the transition, accept the reality, and begin shifting from complaining to seeing themselves as able to cope with the change, although there still may be some stress.
3. Beginnings: There is a new start and commitment to the future; even though letting go may not have been easy, there is training and support that can help.

This theory can apply to any type of change, including my professional transition from a teacher to an education leader. Unfreezing (ending) involves recognizing the need for change and creating an environment that encourages it. This part of the process was crucial for me to transition because I had to leave a familiar environment in the classroom as I moved into a dean role overseeing many programs and faculty more than twice my age. I had to be open to new ideas and concepts while embracing the changes to be made. Moving to the new state (neutral zone) required significant research and preparation. I had to explore what a successful education leader looks like and what my vision was for the role. I also had to get up to speed on the current trends in educational leadership and identify what skills and knowledge I needed to be successful. Learning from other existing leaders and attending conferences could speed up my effectiveness.

Refreezing (beginnings) the new state was about making sure the changes were taking root and that I was continuing to build my leadership skills. I had to ensure my actions aligned with my vision and that I was taking ownership of my transition. I also had to stay focused, motivated, and flexible to truly become an education leader. Finally, evaluating the changes was essential to ensure I was on the right track and making the most of this transition. I had to be honest with myself about whether I was meeting my goals and if I felt the changes I was making were truly benefiting me and my career. While there are many other change models, here are two other ones that are slightly more detailed:

1. *Kotter's (1996) 8-Step Change Model:* This eight-step process helps create a sense of urgency, form a powerful coalition, develop a vision and strategy, communicate the change, empower employees to act, create short-term wins, build on the change, and make the change sustainable. This model focuses on a top-down approach and is highly effective for organizations that need to transition quickly and efficiently.

2. *Hiatt's (2006) Prosci's ADKAR Model:* This is a five-step model that represents an acronym for the steps: to create **Awareness** of the need for change, create the **Desire** to take part in the change, acquire **Knowledge** and skills to support the change, develop the **Ability** to apply the change, and **Reinforce** the change. This is a bottom-up approach to change management that focuses on the individual level of change to help individuals transition from their current state to the desired future state, and it is best suited for organizations that are dealing with multiple stakeholders and are looking to ensure widespread adoption of the change.

It is important to consider the particular context and objectives of the change process to determine the most applicable change management strategy for education leaders. For example, if the aim is to create a culture of collaboration and innovation, then the ADKAR model might be the most appropriate. If the goal is to improve organizational performance, then the Kotter 8-Step Change Model might be the most suitable. Ultimately, all change management strategies have their strengths and weaknesses, and the most appropriate strategy will depend on the context and objectives of the change process. It is important to consult with your team to determine the most suitable change management strategy and ensure it is properly implemented within your organization.

Regarding change management, several of the more popular strategies include training and development, communication strategies, and organizational culture changes. Training and development help create an environment of learning and development, allowing employees to understand the desired objectives of the change. Communication strategies provide a forum for stakeholders to ask questions and provide feedback, helping ensure that goals are met. Finally, organizational culture changes involve reshaping attitudes and practices, inspiring collaboration and innovation.

For change management in education, several strategies are most applicable. These include creating a clear vision of the desired change, engaging stakeholders in the planning process, introducing new processes and technologies, and empowering teachers and staff to act as change champions. It is also important to consider the various stakeholders involved, including students, parents, and teachers. By considering all stakeholders, education leaders can ensure that we implement the desired change in the most effective manner.

In sum, change management is essential for success in education, and there are many strategies that should be considered. Training and development, communication strategies, and organizational culture changes are the most popular strategies, while strategies such as creating a clear vision, engaging stakeholders, introducing new processes, and empowering teachers and staff are the most applicable for education leaders. With the right strategies in place, leaders in education can successfully implement the desired changes to achieve their desired outcomes.

## Resources

**Book:** Heath, C., & Heath, D. (2010). Switch: How to Change Things When Change Is Hard. Crown Business.

**Book:** Johnson, S. (1998). Who Moved My Cheese?: An Amazing Way to Deal with Change in Your Work and in Your Life. G.P. Putnam's Sons.

**Book:** Scott, C., & Jaffe, D. (2005). Managing Change at Work: Leading People Through Organizational Transitions. Crisp Publications.

"Six Keys to Leading Positive Change" – Rosabeth Moss Kanter
https://www.youtube.com/watch?v=owU5aTNPJbs

"The Heart of Change" – John Kotter
https://www.youtube.com/watch?v=1NKti9MyAAw

## Reflection Questions

1. How do I view change? Do I embrace it or prefer the status quo?

   _____

   _____

   _____

   _____

   _____

2. How can I communicate change effectively to stakeholders in my educational community?

   _____

   _____

   _____

   _____

3. How can I ensure that all members of my educational community are prepared and equipped to handle change?

   _____

   _____

   _____

   _____

   _____

4. How can I minimize the resistance to change?

   _____

   _____

   _____

   _____

5.  What change management model would be best to lead change in my institution and have it stick?

    _____

    _____

    _____

    _____

    _____

6.  What specific changes would make the biggest difference in improving my institution?

    _____

    _____

    _____

    _____

    _____

7.  How would I ensure the success of a change initiative at my institution?

    _____

    _____

    _____

    _____

    _____

## Collaboration

Collaboration is your ability to develop the skills and knowledge needed to work effectively with others, specifically up, down, across, and outside the organization. It includes the ability to build and maintain positive working relationships.

On a scale of 1–5, how well do you think you collaborate? Where can you stretch yourself? Do you share information and resources, or do you keep information to yourself? Can others rely upon you to participate and remain engaged in projects until completion? Do you consistently do your best work every day? Are you known for ensuring things are done on time? Do you remain positive when you are in group settings? Do you come prepared for meetings and ready to work? Do you help team members problem solve and allow others to contribute? Are you aware of your behavior in a group setting? Do you listen to others and allow everyone to take part? Can you adjust from leader to follower when needed? Finally, do you take time for self-reflection?

Napoleon Hill has been quoted, "You can succeed best and quickest by helping others succeed." When you think about this quote, where have you helped others succeed? Consider writing five names of people you would like to collaborate with and the purpose of the collaboration. Now reach out to them.

As a leader, it is important to model for your team how to collaborate and the benefits of collaboration. Consider one of your next staff meetings or professional development days to create three scenarios for your team.

You are part of a higher education interdisciplinary team and charged with presenting a solutions-based proposal.

There is some frustration with underperforming staff members on the team.

As the manager, you want to use due process and are not sure what to do. This seems to be an issue across the system.

Then, answer the following scenario questions in small groups:

1. What is the purpose of the team?

   _____

   _____

   _____

   _____

   _____

2.  Who should be included on the team?

_____

_____

_____

_____

_____

3.  What solutions are feasible?

_____

_____

_____

_____

_____

4.  How will I measure success?

_____

_____

_____

_____

_____

In the report-outs by group, listen for any missed opportunities.

While collaboration takes more time, in the long run, it is worth it. According to Ribeiro (2020), the benefits include problem-solving, open communication, adaptability, engagement, and goal alignment.

**Resource**

Ribeiro, S. (2020). Retrieved on April 15, 2023, from https://blog.flock.com/benefits-team-collaboration-work#:~:text=Why%20is%20collaboration%20important%3F,each%20other%20 reach%20your%20goals.

**Reflection Questions**

1. On a scale of 1–5 (where 1 is "not at all" and 5 is "extremely"), how well do I think I collaborate?

   _____

   _____

   _____

   _____

   _____

2. Where can I stretch myself?

   _____

   _____

   _____

   _____

   _____

3. Do I share information and resources, or do I keep information to myself?

   _____

   _____

   _____

   _____

   _____

4. Can others rely on me to take part and remain engaged in projects until they are completed?

   _____

   _____

   _____

   _____

   _____

5. Do I consistently do my best work every day? Am I known for ensuring things are done on time?

_____

_____

_____

_____

_____

6. Do I remain positive when I'm in group settings?

_____

_____

_____

_____

_____

7. Do I come prepared for meetings and ready to work?

_____

_____

_____

_____

_____

8. Do I help team members problem solve and allow others to contribute?

_____

_____

_____

_____

9. Am I aware of my behavior in group settings?

_____

_____

_____

_____

_____

10. Do I listen to others and allow everyone to take part?

_____

_____

_____

_____

_____

11. Can I adjust from leader to follower when needed?

_____

_____

_____

_____

_____

## Communication

If we teach you how to perform better as a leader but do not bolster your communication skills so that you can have greater influence, we are leaving out a vital piece of the puzzle. Studies have consistently shown that the ability to communicate effectively is one of the most important skills for a variety of reasons, especially promotability (Awamleh and Gardner, 1999; Riggio et al. 2003).

Communication is fundamental to leadership because leaders are constantly communicating at all organizational levels within their organizations and to their constituents outside of it. As leaders in education, effective communication is key to our success. We must be able to communicate with our students, colleagues, and community in order to create a positive learning environment. Effective communication can also help us foster better relationships with other educational institutions, which can be beneficial in terms of collaboration and resource sharing.

While there are many elements of communication for the sake of this chapter, we are going to focus on a few key aspects that are critical to building a strong school culture where we consider the needs of others. With all the challenges facing an education leader, we need a process to understand the goals and values of each individual and what influences other's decision making or buy in. We also need to quickly gain insight into what communication strategies will promote influence and lead to the best outcomes. This is important because the traditional education we received in communication is a one size fits all approach.

There are some tried-and-true methods, such as asking open-ended questions and active listening. Listening is a key component of effective communication, and it's especially important in the classroom. We must listen attentively to our students and be able to respond in a way that shows that we've heard and understood them. By connecting with students, we can help enhance learning and their level of engagement. As educators, it's important to make sure that all voices are heard and respected. We must consider the unique perspectives of our students and colleagues in order to ensure that everyone is included in the conversation. However, traditional active listening may lack personalization that allows us to really understand who we are interacting with, what they value, and what influences their agreement on various ideas. This is where emotionally intelligent communication and understanding the values of each person can pave the way to have a great impact.

**So, what is emotional intelligence, and why does it matter?**

Emotional intelligence (EI) is at the core of powerful communication. According to Dr. Daniel Goleman, emotional intelligence is the ability to understand and manage your own emotions and feelings and understand others and how to influence them as well. Goleman identified 5 characteristics of emotional intelligence. They are:

- Self-awareness
- Self-regulation

- Motivation
- Empathy
- Social skills

When we communicate with emotional intelligence, we can empathize with others. This is a critical aspect of building trust, which is important especially with high-stakes conversations that relate to poorly performing people or aspects of organizational effectiveness. When we can discover what makes others tick, we can enhance our ability to connect with them. Historically, understanding others has been approached by asking questions and learning from patterns of interactions. However, there is a system we can use to help us quickly identify the values of others so that we communicate with them in a way that is meaningful to and understood by them.

## Enhancing Your Communication Skills using the B.A.N.K. System

Over 20 years ago, the B.A.N.K. Methodology was created by Cheri Tree, an international best-selling author and the Founder and CEO of Codebreaker Technologies, as a reliable way to increase sales. Tree was working in sales at the time and, in her own words, wasn't very good at it. That's when she studied the buying behavior of her prospects and customers. The system she developed to assess the personality type of her prospects and clients in just 90 seconds had a dramatic impact on her sales success. What is unique about this method is that unlike most personality systems that focus on understanding psychological characteristics or traits of the person taking the assessment, this system was created to understand who the customer or client is and what influences their decision making or buying behavior. San Francisco State University (SFSU) validated the B.A.N.K. Methodology, and it was Dr. Ryan T. Howell, who was then an Associate Professor of Psychology and Statistics Professor at SFSU who concluded, "The B.A.N.K. Code Assessment is a quick reliable and valid measure that predicts buying behavior and increases your probability of closing the sale." (Howell, R. T., & Tree, C., 2015)

Throughout the last 20 years, more and more people have been introduced to and used the B.A.N.K. Methodology to improve their sales. The unexpected side effect of using the system is that users began reporting improvement in both personal and professional relationships all because they were using the 90 second assessment to discover the personality code of the people in their lives. Users reported marriages were saved, suicides avoided, and relationships in families were improving. All of this occurred through the use of B.A.N.K. which is now considered as a lens through which to understand others and build strong relationships, increasing one's emotional intelligence.

## Why Do Educators Need To Understand Sales?

Educators are always selling. We may not be selling cars or widgets, but we are selling information and opportunities for engagement. As leaders, we are constantly selling ideas and concepts to gain the buy-in of others to achieve things. Even Mary Parker Follett once said that management is the "art of getting things done through other people". So as an academic leader, you may sell many things, from improving the student experience, new initiatives, and programs, improving retention and creating a better learning experience.

Many times, the information we have to share may not be positive. Education professionals need to be comfortable selling - or influencing - the outcome of a conversation. And we can do this best when we understand the personality type of others. Whether we are a teacher or a leader we are focused on educating others in order to enhance their performance.

If we want to communicate with influence, we need to forget the Golden Rule - "Treat others as you would like to be treated." Of course, we all want to be treated with dignity and respect; that is a given. But beyond that, it is important not to approach or communicate with others in the way we like to be treated, but to "treat them how they want to be treated", the Platinum Rule. So how do others like to be treated? That can be a challenging question, as we all are unique and have personal preferences as well.

**About The Personality Codes**

As detailed in the book Why They Buy (Tree, C., 2017) there are four primary personality codes: Blueprint, Action, Nurturing, and Knowledge. Each has different values, buying behaviors and different motivations for buying that are reliable. An important thing to note is that every person has all four codes within them: just to varying degrees. Unlike other personality assessments, this framework assumes people can learn and grow since personality isn't permanent. This system honors and respects each personality code, recognizing that each code has strengths that will contribute to unique perspectives. Understanding the personality codes has major implications for your own learning and helping others learn. So, whether you are applying this information to accelerate your own learning on your leadership path or helping teachers and students to teach and learn more effectively, applying this powerful information will create a learning environment that fosters growth.

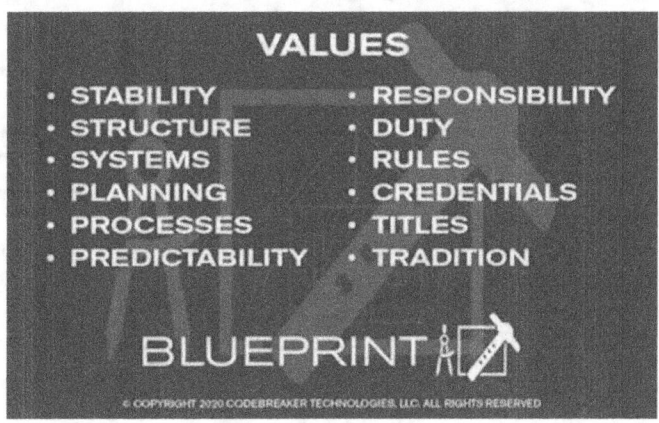

The Blueprint Personality Type is characterized as being "inside the box." They enjoy step-by-step processes, systems, rules, predictability, and structure. They are motivated to avoid risk at all costs. This group will learn best with a step-by-step system that is presented in an organized way. They have a strong sense of duty and responsibility and will keep their commitments when they understand the risk of not doing so.

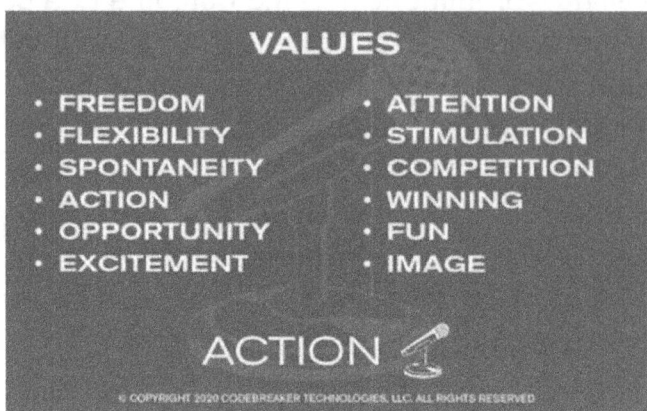

The Action Personality Type is characterized as being "outside the box." They enjoy opportunity, winning, flexibility, competition, and fun. We motivate them to win. This group learns best with bullet-point style information. Get right to the bottom line and don't provide too many details, charts, or information. They want to know who, what, why and how. Too much information will turn them off.

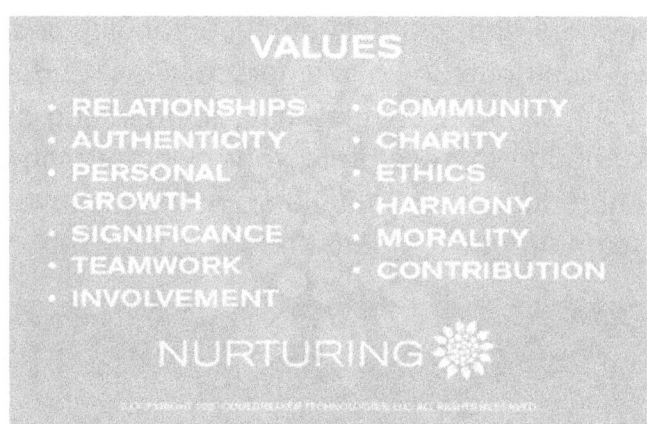

The Nurturing Personality Type wants to "recycle the box." They enjoy authenticity, relationships, teamwork, community, and contribution. We motivate them to make a difference. This group wants to feel they are part of the team. Involve them in decision making and other school activities as it will help them to contribute to their community.

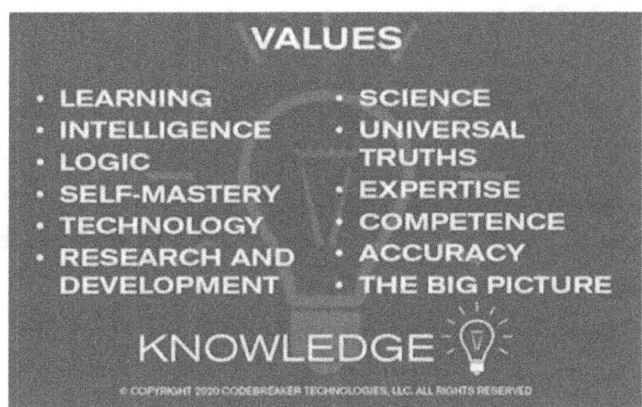

The Knowledge Personality Type "designed the box." They enjoy learning, self-mastery, science, universal truths, and understanding the big picture. They are motivated by always being right; therefore, they decide slowly and carefully to avoid being wrong. This group needs to understand the big picture. They want details and as much information as possible. They will be skeptical and will always ask questions. They need time to process new information and will not decide quickly.

As a school, there is an online system that you may license to provide these reports to all of your students and other stakeholders. At the same time that this report is provided to someone, there is a parallel report that is simultaneously generated that provides insights to the school on how best to communicate and influence each person.

To get your complimentary report in less than 90 seconds please visit: www.crackmycode. com/learn

To get a custom link for your organization contact: Dr. Eric Goodman at eric@highered-change.com

## Is Having This Type of Report Manipulation?

The answer is no. Understanding the personality code merely provides us with insight regarding how someone will best receive and understand our message. Nothing is as critical for learning as understanding the message. It allows us to present new information in the best way possible the first time, avoid misunderstandings, and avoid feeling like others "just don't get it, "just don't care," or "just won't listen."

When we communicate with a Knowledge personality type the same way we communicate with an Action personality type we may actually turn off the person in the process. This type of one size fits all communication results in our message either not being understood or heard. However, when we incorporate using the B.A.N.K code into our daily approach, we can communicate with others in a structured way that can predictably enhance the quality of learning and our relationships.

ERIC GOODMAN, Ph.D., and KIM NUGENT, Ed.D.

**Benefits Of Communicating With Emotional Intelligence and Using the BANKCODE**

Insight and empathy are the two biggest benefits of communicating with emotional intelligence and knowledge of the BANKCODE. When we can begin conversations with others with insight into how they learn and think as well as what they value, we interact with others with compassion and empathy. We gain a tremendous amount of trust when we can sit with someone else with no judgment of right or wrong and without attaching ourselves to any emotionally charged communication. We can simply be present and serve others at a higher level than ever before.

**How To Get Started With The B.A.N.K. Methodology**

The first step to getting started with B.A.N.K. is to determine your own code and get your Complimentary Personal Profile Report. Once again, this report will reveal your personality code, values and traits. Keep in mind that emotional intelligence has an intrapersonal and interpersonal aspect so the first step to understanding another person is to know yourself.

After you have received your complimentary personality report please take a few minutes to complete this advanced 20-item personality assessment so you can determine your relative score for each personality type of the B.A.N.K. system. This will provide you with more insight as you reflect on your complimentary personality report that you receive digitally.

# WHICH PERSONALITY TYPE ARE YOU?

On a scale of 1 to 5 where 1 is *almost never* and 5 is *always*, rate the following questions.

| | | | | | |
|---|---|---|---|---|---|
| 1. I look for opportunities to serve and help others. | 1 | 2 | 3 | 4 | 5 |
| 2. I embrace risk. | 1 | 2 | 3 | 4 | 5 |
| 3. I believe that it is important that rules are enforced. | 1 | 2 | 3 | 4 | 5 |
| 4. I highly value competence. | 1 | 2 | 3 | 4 | 5 |
| 5. I value predictability in my life. | 1 | 2 | 3 | 4 | 5 |
| 6. I make decisions based on good analysis and good data. | 1 | 2 | 3 | 4 | 5 |
| 7. I tend to be compassionate and tender to most people. | 1 | 2 | 3 | 4 | 5 |
| 8. I need to be the leader. | 1 | 2 | 3 | 4 | 5 |
| 9. I find joy in charitable giving. | 1 | 2 | 3 | 4 | 5 |
| 10. I prefer having a step-by-step system to follow. | 1 | 2 | 3 | 4 | 5 |
| 11. I place great value on expertise. | 1 | 2 | 3 | 4 | 5 |
| 12. I like to be the center of attention. | 1 | 2 | 3 | 4 | 5 |
| 13. I crave stimulation and excitement. | 1 | 2 | 3 | 4 | 5 |
| 14. I highly value intelligence. | 1 | 2 | 3 | 4 | 5 |
| 15. I am passionate about supporting the causes that I believe in. | 1 | 2 | 3 | 4 | 5 |
| 16. I am disciplined and like to follow protocols, guidelines and timelines. | 1 | 2 | 3 | 4 | 5 |
| 17. I crave a lifestyle of fame and fortune. | 1 | 2 | 3 | 4 | 5 |
| 18. I value science and the scientific method. | 1 | 2 | 3 | 4 | 5 |
| 19. I value stability over change. | 1 | 2 | 3 | 4 | 5 |
| 20. It is important for me to make deep connections with other people. | 1 | 2 | 3 | 4 | 5 |

HIGHER ED CHANGE, L.L.C.
HIGHEREDGECHANGE.COM | ERIC@HIGHEREDGECHANGE.COM

# PERSONALITY ASSESSMENT SCORING GUIDE

1.  Complete your answers in the score grid below based on the corresponding question. For example, the answer to question 1 belongs in the NURTURING column next to the number 1.

2.  For each B.A.N.K. Personality Type, add the values in each column for a score out of 25.

3.  YOUR **BANK**CODE starts with your highest score and ends with your lowest. In case of a tie, you may choose which code to put first.

| # | BLUEPRINT | # | ACTION | # | NURTURING | # | KNOWLEDGE |
|---|-----------|---|--------|---|-----------|---|-----------|
| 3 | | 2 | | 1 | | 4 | |
| 5 | | 8 | | 7 | | 6 | |
| 10 | | 12 | | 9 | | 11 | |
| 16 | | 13 | | 15 | | 14 | |
| 19 | | 17 | | 20 | | 18 | |
| TOTALS B | /25 | A | /25 | N | /25 | K | /25 |

## YOUR BANKCODE

**HIGH SCORE** [ ] [ ] [ ] [ ] **LOW SCORE**

1st      2nd      3rd      4th

### HOW TO INTERPRET YOUR SCORE

25 out of 25 shows a very passionate, intense point of view, while a score under 12 shows a lack of passion or even an aversion towards that personality type.

To schedule an appointment to learn more about how the B.A.N.K. Methodology can help you improve the culture and outcomes within your organization, schedule a complimentary consultation with Dr. Eric Goodman who may be reached at eric@higheredchange.com. This system may be integrated through the entire school and student experience in every area from admissions, athletics, financial aid, faculty, advising, career services, residential life, student services, etc. Ultimately, this system will help build a connected school culture that will improve student engagement, learning, retention and other outcomes.

## Resources:

**Book:** Carnegie, D. (1936) How to Win Friends and Influence People, Simon & Schuster.

**Book:** Patterson, K., Grenny, J., McMillan, R., & Switzler, A. (2012). Crucial Conversations: Tools for Talking When Stakes Are High (2nd ed.). McGraw-Hill Education.

**Book:** Tree, C. (2017). Why They Buy: Cracking the Personality Code to Achieve Record Sales and Real Wealth. Aviva Publishing.

Start with why – Simon Sinek –
https://www.youtube.com/watch?v=u4ZoJKF_VuA

How to speak so people will want to listen – Julian Treasure
https://www.youtube.com/watch?v=elho2S0Zahl

**Reflection Questions:**

1.  How can I improve my active listening skills to better understand the needs and perspectives of others?

   _____

   _____

   _____

   _____

   _____

2.  How can I adjust my communication style to be more effective with different personalities and learning styles?

   _____

   _____

   _____

   _____

   _____

3.  How can I use communication to build trust and establish positive relationships with others?

   _____

   _____

   _____

   _____

   _____

4.  How do I communicate with different stakeholders in my education setting (students, parents, colleagues, administrators, etc.)?

   _____

   _____

   _____

   _____

   _____

5.  How can I improve my communication skills?

_____

_____

_____

_____

_____

## Conflict Resolution

Conflict resolution is learning how to effectively resolve conflicts that arise within an organization, which will happen. It is inevitable and cannot be avoided. When in leadership, there is an expectation for you to handle conflict well and not avoid it. For some people, this is going to require training and development. Ignoring conflict does not make it better; it actually gets worse over time and can spiral out of control. It can damage entire departments by creating increased tension. This is true in professional and personal situations. It is unrealistic to accommodate everyone and expect everyone to get along all the time. According to Korn Ferry (2015, p. 67), skilled behavior in this area includes the ability to read situations carefully, being good at focused listening, and settling disagreements quickly while finding common ground resulting in cooperation. In addition, Korn Ferry found managers were spending 18 percent of their time dealing with direct face-to-face conflict (2015, p. 68).

If conflict arises between two team members, sit down with each of them individually first to determine the actual issue. The reality is it could be a difference of opinion, a difference in personality or goal alignment, a misunderstanding, and hurt feelings. What is the perception of the situation? What happened? Ask clarifying questions. Ask for an example. What might be a viable solution? What is the impact? Listen to their words. Notice their body language. Take notes. Allow them to express their emotions. Sometimes this helps to de-escalate the situation. Make them feel comfortable with the information they are sharing with you.

Once clear on the issue(s), bring the two staff or faculty members together. Allow them to hash out the differences in a safe and neutral environment. Seize on points of common agreement. Certainly, there will be different perceptions, and your role will be to help them create a win-win solution.

After the group meeting, continue to monitor each of them and follow up. This additional step will create a positive and healthy work environment if the conflict persists. Going to another third party or a mediator can also aid these situations.

Conflict is healthy; in the end, you may achieve a better outcome by listening to all parties. Many effective leaders have turned conflict into learning opportunities and innovation. We hope you will be one of those leaders.

**Resource**

**Book:** Korn Ferry. (2015). The skills of conflict management. New York, NY: Korn Ferry.

## Reflection Questions

1. Am I competent in conflict resolution, or am I conflict averse?

_____

_____

_____

_____

_____

2. What is my plan to gain more competency in further developing my conflict resolution skills to stretch myself?

_____

_____

_____

_____

_____

3. What strategies do I use?

_____

_____

_____

_____

_____

## Decision-Making

As educational leaders, we are obligated to make knowledgeable, impactful decisions that benefit our students, staff, and organization. Decision-making is essential to any leader's role, as it decides the path and accomplishment of their initiatives. Although decision-making can be hard and challenging, it is important to consider whether the decision is correct, considering various points of view. Is it the correct move for the students? Is it the correct move for the employers? For the community? For faculty and staff? By considering these angles, we can arrive at more effective decisions that benefit everyone involved.

Educators must be mindful of their duties and make informed decisions that will bring success. Knowledge, skill, and experience are required to make effective choices. To carry out this, leaders must comprehend the value of obtaining the relevant data, examine it thoroughly, and consider the potential effects of their decisions. They ought to be acquainted with the resources at hand to support decision-making.

One of the most important aspects of decision-making is considering the potential risks. Education leaders should carefully consider the potential outcomes of any decision they make and weigh the benefits and risks associated with each option. A wide range of conditions affects each decision from the certainty/uncertainty or risk standpoint.

While there are several decision-making models, the choice of a model/approach ultimately depends on the leader's preference and sometimes other political factors. Perhaps the most common model is based on economic assumptions and the notion that the decision will be logical in the organization's best economic interests.

Another model often seen, especially when the environment is uncertain and complex where people may pursue different goals, falls into a political approach. In these situations, leaders may disagree and engage in a push-and-pull debate, sometimes bargaining or compromising based on various alliances that support a specific goal. As a new leader, it is very important to understand the political landscape, so to speak, along with the likely positions of the formal and informal leaders in the organization. Regardless of the context, it is advisable to determine the criteria and the parameters for the decision, as well as who will be involved in the decision-making process.

Education leaders should also be conscious of their decisions regarding the resources at their disposal. Decisions need to be made in a way that maximizes the use of the resources available while also considering the effects of their decisions on the long-term sustainability of their organization. In addition, education leaders need to be aware of the external environment in which they are operating. They need to be mindful of the external pressures that might influence their decisions and the potential implications of their decisions on their organization.

Finally, education leaders should use the data available to them to inform their decision-making. By understanding the available data, leaders can make more informed decisions leading to better outcomes for their organization. We all have a responsibility to make informed decisions that will positively impact our students, staff, and institution. By understanding the keys to making effective decisions, education leaders can ensure that their decisions will have a lasting and positive effect.

No discussion of decision-making would be complete without considering the decision-making process. The decision-making process involves identifying problems and opportunities and ultimately taking action. As human beings, we face many questions or, rather, decision points in our lives. Whether it is a complicated decision in the school setting or simply choosing what project to prioritize, there isn't a day that goes by when we are not deciding. The ability to choose from various alternatives is part of the human experience and what separates us from other living species. At its core, the decision-making process involves gathering information, analyzing it, and making a decision based on that analysis. At each stage, it is important to consider the decision's impact on the business, its stakeholders, and the overall environment. We need to understand the steps involved in this process in order to make the best decisions possible.

Making decisions is a vital part of daily living, and by following certain steps, we can help ensure that our decisions are reasonable. To make effective decisions, we can pursue some traditional steps in the process:

1. *Recognize the issue.* Before making any decision, decision-makers must have an unmistakable comprehension of the issue they are tending to and the potential arrangements. To gain this understanding, it is important to do research, assess applicable records, and gather input from specialists or stakeholders to get a thorough understanding of the environment, along with an awareness of past and present patterns and the capacity for change.

2. *Consider the consequences.* All decisions have consequences, and education leaders must consider the potential effects of their decisions on their students, staff, and the overall organization. It is also important to consider the interests of multiple stakeholders and the varying perspectives of parents and other community members. A thorough data analysis is also essential to ensure the best possible outcome. Remember to be mindful of the cost and risk associated with the decision. While it is important to consider the potential benefits of a decision, it is also important to assess all the associated costs and risks, which can often be overlooked.

3. *Involve key stakeholders.* To ensure that the decision is made in the organization's best interest, it is important to involve key stakeholders in the decision-making process. This includes parents, teachers, staff, and other community members. It is also important to ensure that the decision-making process is transparent and that all stakeholders are informed and consulted in a timely manner.

4. *Be open to feedback.* Education leaders must be open to feedback from stakeholders and be willing to consider different perspectives on the issue. They must adjust their decision based on input from those involved. It is important to generate a list of alternatives that involves considering the different options available and their potential

outcomes. As you capture this feedback, you may then evaluate the alternatives. This includes assessing each option's strengths, weaknesses, opportunities, and threats.

5. *Take action.* After careful consideration, education leaders must take action to implement the decision. This includes ensuring that stakeholders are informed of the decision and that the steps are taken to implement the decision. To take action, you must have the resources and support to ensure that the decision is efficiently implemented. It is also important to review the decision regularly to ensure it is still appropriate for the context and make any necessary adjustments.

By following these five steps, education leaders can ensure they are making effective decisions that consider the needs and interests of their students, staff, and stakeholders. With a clear understanding of the problem, careful consideration of the consequences, involvement of key stakeholders, openness to feedback, and taking action, education leaders can ensure they are making decisions that are in the best interest of their organization.

## Resources

**Book:** Dobelli, R. (2013). The Art of Thinking Clearly. HarperCollins.

**Book:** Heath, C., & Heath, D. (2013). Decisive: How to Make Better Choices in Life and Work. Crown Business.

**Book:** Kahneman, D. (2011). Thinking, Fast and Slow. Farrar, Straus and Giroux.

MindTools – PDCA model
https://www.mindtools.com/as2l5i1/pdca-plan-do-check-act

"Why We Make Bad Decisions" – Dan Gilbert
https://www.youtube.com/watch?v=c-4flnuxNV4

"Are We in Control of Our Decisions?" – Dan Ariely https://www.youtube.com/watch?v=9X68dm92HVl

**Reflection Questions**

1. How do I currently approach decision-making?

   _____

   _____

   _____

   _____

   _____

2. How can I involve others in the decision-making process to ensure diverse perspectives are considered?

   _____

   _____

   _____

   _____

3. What are some strategies I can use to manage uncertainty and risk in my decision-making?

   _____

   _____

   _____

   _____

   _____

4. How can I balance short-term and long-term goals in my decision-making?

   _____

   _____

   _____

   _____

5. How can I continue to improve my decision-making skills over time?

   _____

   _____

   _____

   _____

# Ethics

It seems most people want to be ethical and do the right thing. However, the right thing can be hard to define, so sometimes even the notion of ethics may be hard to define. However, ethics is considered the code of moral principles and values that governs the behaviors of a person or group regarding what is right or wrong. So, it is easy to think of ethics as set internal values or standards.

Please consider your ethical standards and whether you'd consider your behavior on a continuum from *always acting ethically* to *never being ethical*. And depending on your view, think about what the gap may be between what you'd like to be doing and what you are doing in practice. As a rule of thumb, please consider the applicability of the Golden Rule when you encounter an ethical decision and ask, "How would I like to be treated in this situation?" While this isn't the Platinum Rule we discussed in the section on communication, the key point is recognizing that regardless of the person, organization, or even broader culture, there are standards that exist either explicitly or implicitly.

Of course, as an educational leader, it is important to recognize your individual values and those inherent in your organization's culture. In education, we have many codified regulations and laws that we must follow to remain in compliance. Without these regulations and laws, we may have choices governed by our free will. Some people mistakenly assume that if it is not illegal, it must be ethical. However, finding the balance based on what is legally and morally acceptable is the key to understanding ethical behavior.

As teachers transition to educational leadership roles, it is important to clearly understand the ethical implications of the role. As a teacher, one of the greatest challenges is to ensure that the students receive the best education possible and that their rights, welfare, and safety are respected. Similarly, ethical classroom teaching issues must be considered when transitioning to an educational leadership role.

The best strategies for ethical leadership in education involve a combination of ethical principles, integrity, and trust. Ethical principles guide how one should act and lead in an educational setting. Integrity is essential, as it shows the willingness to act in the best interest of the students and the school. Finally, trust is the foundation of any successful educational setting, as it allows teachers and students to share ideas, be honest with one another, and understand the importance of mutual respect and understanding.

As a teacher, you may have recognized the importance of creating psychological safety. It is worth discussing how psychological safety translates from the classroom into the organizational environment. To have an ethical culture, it is critical to create an environment of trust, respect, and openness. Without psychological safety, students and employees may feel threatened to share feedback or identify unethical behaviors that are taking place. Of course, this prevents students from taking risks and trying new ideas in the classroom.

In the same way you want to establish an environment that encourages students to feel comfortable sharing their thoughts and ideas without fear of criticism or judgment, you need to set that same tone in your school. People need to speak up about ethical situations without fear of negative consequences. In an environment of psychological safety, people will be less willing to relent to others' opinions, especially if they question them, compromise the truth, take shortcuts, or make quick emotion-based decisions.

The bottom line is when employees feel comfortable speaking up, it can lead to better decision-making and improved ethical behavior, which is essential for creating a positive company culture.

As a leader, it is important to recognize the Golden Rule and the standards that need to be followed and know if there is a commitment to following them. Ultimately, a leader needs to have a moral compass that helps them act with integrity no matter who is watching.

As an undergraduate, I remember taking a business ethics course. The professor shared a litmus test that you could apply to evaluate your actions. If what you are about to do was on the front page of the *New York Times*, would you be proud of that? Or is there something you must hide? In this day of ubiquitous video access, if you imagine that all your actions are being recorded, would you want others to watch your behavior? All outstanding leaders have clear values that serve as the foundation in guiding their decisions, especially during challenging times.

Besides these strategies, education leaders should know the ethical implications of their role. This involves understanding and respecting the rights, welfare, and safety of students, as well as the policies of the school. It also involves being aware of the potential conflicts of interest that may arise and understanding how to handle them ethically. Education leaders should also practice self-reflection, allowing them to realize their values and beliefs and how they may affect their decision-making. As a leader, you will face situations that require courage, especially to do the right thing in the face of disagreement or other outside pressures.

There may be times when you face a tough decision, such as trimming the budget or closing an academic program; there is risk, and others' lives will be affected. As an academic leader, making ethical decisions is paramount to upholding the values of the institution you lead.

The following steps should be taken to ensure that you make sound ethical decisions.

1. *Become knowledgeable about ethical considerations.* Start by understanding the core ethical principles that apply to the decision you're making. This includes understanding the implications of any potential decision and the consequences of any ethical violations.

2. *Assess the situation.* Evaluate the facts and circumstances of the situation and identify potential risks or ethical dilemmas. Consider the potential effect of any decision on all stakeholders involved.

3. *Identify key stakeholders.* Identify all stakeholders who could be affected by the decision you make and consider their perspectives.

4. *Consult with experts.* Discuss the issue with experts in the field to get their insights and perspective.

5. *Decide.* Considering all the information you've gathered, make a decision that you feel is ethically sound.

6. *Reassess*. Once the decision has been made, take the time to reassess the situation and evaluate the outcome.

By following these steps, academic leaders can be confident that they are making ethical decisions that will protect the institution's values and ensure everyone is treated fairly.

As the world advances, we are obliged as educational leaders to comprehend our duty to nature and society. This obligation, also called social responsibility, concerns moral choice-making and requires an organization to consider the consequences of its activities. When settling on ethical choices, we must consider their effect on our stakeholders, the environment, and the worldwide network. This incorporates thinking about the immediate and long term potential harm our choices can cause. We must help ensure that the choices align with our school's mission and qualities.

Regarding social responsibility, organizations must comprehend the effect of their choices on employees, students, stakeholders, and the environment. This incorporates considering how their choices may influence the well-being, security, and welfare of others. By having a clear understanding of the ethical implications of the role and the strategies for ethical leadership in education, teachers transitioning to an educational leadership role can ensure that the students and school receive the best possible educational experience.

## Resources

**Book:** Ferrell, O. C., Fraedrich, J., & Ferrell, L. (2018). Business Ethics: Ethical Decision Making and Cases. Cengage Learning.

**Book:** Shapiro, J. P., & Stefkovich, J. A. (2022). Ethical Leadership and Decision Making in Education: Applying Theoretical Perspectives to Complex Dilemmas (5th ed.). Routledge.

**Book:** Singer, P. (2011). Practical Ethics. Cambridge University Press.

"The Do's and Don'ts of Educational Leadership" – Pedro Noguera
https://www.youtube.com/watch?v=upT0oy-kKz4

FROM TEACHER TO LEADER

## Reflection Questions

1. How do my personal values and beliefs impact my decision-making in the institution?

   _____

   _____

   _____

   _____

   _____

2. In what ways can I ensure that all students are treated fairly and equitably in my institution?

   _____

   _____

   _____

   _____

   _____

3. How do I handle ethical dilemmas or conflicts that arise in my work as an educator?

   _____

   _____

   _____

   _____

   _____

4. How can I teach and model ethical behavior for my students and staff?

   _____

   _____

   _____

   _____

5. How do I prioritize ethical considerations when deciding? Do I prioritize short-term gains over long-term ethical considerations?

   _____

   _____

   _____

   _____

## Faculty Development

If you are a new leader, you may not know what your organization provides concerning faculty development opportunities, so inquire. Your organization may have access to online training. They may offer face-to-face professional development days, or they might offer nothing, and it could be your opportunity to bring new resources and training to your organization. The organization may have a faculty development director on staff.

Many years ago, I presented at a national conference and titled my presentation "The True Cost of Faculty Development." We can assure you that if your organization is not offering faculty development training, it costs your students. Students have a low tolerance for poor teaching and vote with their feet and, many times, either drop the class or withdraw from school if they don't like the teaching. While teachers in the K-12 arena get much training in this area, this is sadly not true in higher education. Most faculty members are hired because of their credentials and subject matter expertise. While this is great, they are often not formally trained in facilitation.

In my past professional experience, I have developed faculty development certification programs from the basic how-to of teaching to advanced learning-centered courses for experienced faculty members. The result was higher student engagement and increased faculty satisfaction and confidence levels. Once we implemented the program, as faculty completed the initial certifications, they could co-teach and ultimately teach the program to new faculty members. I have also supported other external organizations' creation of a curriculum or program for faculty development for both face-to-face and online courses. Nothing gives me more joy than making a difference in faculty members' professional lives and seeing it put into action in the classroom.

Consider offering faculty development training after a required new employee orientation. This is even more important today, and organizations have pivoted to online, hybrid, from face-to-face classes. Faculty had to quickly learn to use the technology and then convert their classes from face-to-face to hybrid or online. The role of teaching and facilitation is more complex than ever, and the generational differences are wider than ever.

One of many effective strategies is to conduct a needs assessment, review student satisfaction surveys, and conduct faculty observations to determine what is needed. Learn who the gifted faculty are and what faculty are struggling with. Be a resource to help them. Consider appointing a buddy or mentor for the first few months to help with the transition.

There are great resources today from consultants specializing in faculty development, online courses, websites, books, podcasts, TED Talks, and so much more. Check out our list of resources to get started.

### Resources

**Book:** Angelo, T. A., & Cross, K. P. (1993). Classroom assessment techniques. Jossey Bass: San Francisco, CA.

**Book:** Meier, D. (2000). The accelerated learning handbook. McGraw Hill: New York, NY.

Confidence in Leadership. [Newsletter]. LinkedIn. https://www.linkedin.com/newsletters/7055727251606155264/

Faculty Focus: Higher Education and Learning. Retrieved from https://www.facultyfocus.com/

Lead like the great conductors. (2009). Retrieved from https://www.ted.com/talks/itay_talgam_lead_like_the_great_conductors

**Professional Services:**

Higher Ed Change, Dr. Eric Goodman, Eric@higheredchange.com or Eric@drericgoodman.com (leadership, faculty and staff development, executive and professional coaching, retention, growth strategies, online learning, academic and student services, curriculum development, competency based education, quality enhancement and accreditation services).

Kim Nugent Enterprises, Dr. Kim Nugent, Nugent1234@gmail.com or kim@ drnugentspeaks.com (faculty development, leadership development, and coaching services provided to increase engagement and retention).

## Reflection Questions

1. What are my strength areas in faculty development?

   _____

   _____

   _____

   _____

   _____

2. What faculty development opportunities are offered at my organization?

   _____

   _____

   _____

   _____

   _____

3. Where are the gaps in faculty development?

   _____

   _____

   _____

   _____

   _____

4. What solutions do I propose?

   _____

   _____

   _____

   _____

   _____

## Influence

Influence refers to the ability to persuade or affect the actions, opinions, or decisions of others. A leader in education needs to understand the importance of influence to effectively lead their team, students, and other stakeholders toward a common goal.

To successfully influence people, you must be able to build support. One of the best ways of doing this, which you may have learned from teaching in the classroom, is to create and maintain relationships with others. While in the classroom setting, you were focused on influencing the learning of students. However, as you develop into a leader in education, it is critical that you think about influencing others who can assist you in achieving your objectives. Keep in mind the earlier discussion about communication and personality styles with the B.A.N.K. Code. Most great communicators have in common certain skills of influence, which they may have developed over the years.

We know from research that people buy from other people who they know, like, and trust, and that happens at a dramatically higher rate when their personality types are aligned. This means that you have a choice to practice the Platinum Rule and treat others how they want to be treated or risk using the Golden Rule and potentially detract from the relationship. When people feel heard and appreciated, the ability to build a trusting relationship is enhanced.

When transitioning from being a teacher to a leader in education, the skill of influence becomes even more essential, although it can be a challenging process. While many skills must be developed to be successful in an educational leadership role, there are a few key strategies that can maximize influence. The first strategy is to listen and understand. Remember, this is a communication skill that we discussed earlier. As Stephen Covey suggested in *The 7 Habits of Highly Effective People*, you must first seek to understand and then be understood. As an education leader, it is important to understand the needs of both teachers and students and to be open to different perspectives.

You also need to build relationships with a wider range of stakeholders, including administrators, board members, and community members. Establishing trust and rapport is crucial for building a sound foundation for influence, meaning listening to all stakeholders and gathering information from various sources. Listening and understanding will help create trust and collaboration when making decisions and implementing policies.

Remember that before you can influence people, you need to align them with your vision or the outcome you're striving for, and you need to know what drives them. As we know, people are driven by their values, which you can quickly identify with a powerful tool like the B.A.N.K. personality system. Whether it is teachers, staff, or other stakeholders, really understanding the needs, preferences, and expectations of others can help a leader align and connect with them.

The second strategy is to communicate clearly and concisely. Clear communication is the key to successful influence. It is important to communicate expectations, objectives, and any changes to the organization clearly and concisely. It is also important to be aware of different communication styles and tailor your approach accordingly.

The third strategy is to be an advocate for change. Education leaders should be open to and support change. They should challenge existing structures and create new ideas that benefit all stakeholders. Advocating for change sets the tone for others to follow and helps encourage collaboration and innovation. In the process of advocating for change, think about how people are likely to react to the proposed change. By anticipating this, you'll have a better opportunity to present your ideas in a manner that addresses any concerns and aligns with others' interests.

The fourth strategy is to build relationships. Building relationships is essential for successful leadership. It is important to build relationships with teachers and students and other education leaders and stakeholders. By building relationships, education leaders can gain insights into different perspectives and use those to make informed decisions. Influence is not just about convincing others to adopt your ideas and opinions. It is also about being strategic in how you approach change. Identify key stakeholders and allies and develop a plan for engaging with them and gaining their support.

Remember to encourage collaboration among different groups and departments within and outside your school. Provide opportunities for input and involvement and recognize and reward contributions. Finally, education leaders should strive to be a model of excellence. Education leaders should lead by example and show the behaviors and actions they want from other stakeholders. As a leader, you need an awareness of what you're communicating, and some say that your actions speak louder than words. You must lead by example, as your behavior sets the tone for the rest of the school. Model the behaviors you want to see in others and be consistent in your actions and words.

It is important to develop your emotional intelligence so you're becoming more aware of your strengths, regulating your emotions and behaviors, and understanding others and how best to influence them with how you interact. Increasing your emotional intelligence will help inspire, motivate, and encourage others to reach their full potential and strive to be their best.

When transitioning from a classroom teacher to an education leader, it is important to remember that teaching and influencing are two sides of the same coin. Classroom teaching can help build relationships, foster collaboration, and create a positive environment. Leadership is a way to use those skills to influence others and create a lasting impact on the organization. By applying these strategies, education leaders can maximize their influence and create a successful organization.

## Resources

**Book**: Cialdini, R. B. (2006). Influence: The Psychology of Persuasion. Harper Business.

**Book:** Cialdini, R.B. (2016). Pre-Suasion: A Revolutionary Way to Influence and Persuade. Simon & Schuster.

**Book:** Finerty, S. Z. (2016). Cross-Functional Influence: Getting Things Done Across the Organization. Apress.

"The Science of Persuasion" – Robert Cialdini https://www.youtube.com/watch?v=cFdCzN7RYbw&t=8s

"How to Influence People" – Tony Robbins
https://www.youtube.com/watch?v=4avhbxaU7gw

**Reflection Questions**

1.  What strategies do I use to influence others?

    _____

    _____

    _____

    _____

    _____

2.  What are some of the key factors that influence people's decisions in education?

    _____

    _____

    _____

    _____

    _____

3.  What are some strategies for minimizing resistance to change through influence that I can use at my institution?

    _____

    _____

    _____

    _____

    _____

4.  What are my strengths and weaknesses when it comes to influence?

    _____

    _____

    _____

    _____

    _____

5.  How can I use my influence to empower and support others?

    _____

    _____

    _____

    _____

    _____

6. How can I continue to develop my influence skills?

_____

_____

_____

_____

_____

## Innovation and Creativity

When I think of innovation and creativity, I am reminded of this quote: "To stay ahead, you must have your next idea waiting in the wings" by Rosabeth Moss Kanter, an American author and academic. The Harvard Professional Development program offers a great YouTube video explaining the difference between convergent and divergent thinking of being able to come up with ideas and explore possibilities. When an organization fosters innovation, it leads to positive organizational change initiatives and manages resistance to change. It is a way to develop new ways to look at problems while creating novel solutions.

When organizations foster innovation, they thrive in a constantly changing landscape. According to *Inc. Magazine*, a study of 1,500 CEOs showed leaders rank creativity/innovation as the top leadership attribute needed for prosperity. It is the one thing that cannot be outsourced. It is the lifeblood of a sustainable competitive advantage.

Nothing kills creativity and innovation more often than when leaders around the table say, "We tried that, and it didn't work," or "Nothing is broken, so why change it?" Some reasons for not cultivating innovation can be risk aversion, not being open to new ideas, being complacent or apathetic, and having a limited creativity toolbox.

According to Ray Anthony (2016), innovative leaders are decisive, driven, and action-oriented change agents. He also describes the characteristics of innovative leaders, such as the ability to beckon a big vision, high-risk tolerance, open-mindedness, elite team builders, confidence and optimism, having fun, heavy engagement with innovators, and offering big and bold concepts and plans.

So how can you foster creativity in a group? Consider generating a list of questions as quickly as you can. Do not generate solutions yet. Take a program or service you are unhappy with and represent it visually. Break it down into pieces. Experiment to find something that might work. Avoid distractions. Allow everyone to take part.

If you want to foster a culture of innovation, be passionate, celebrate ideas, foster autonomy, encourage courage, fail forward, and maximize diversity (Linker 2011). Strategies can include mind mapping, freewriting, or sticky-note problem-solving, to name a few.

Innovation happens one step at a time. When you think about the great innovators over time, they were not overnight successes. They tried many times repeatedly until they realized the great next new product or service. They did not do it alone. Who do you admire? What can you learn from them? How can you bring this approach to your next meeting?

### Resources

**Book:** Linkner, J. (2011). The innovator's DNA: Mastering the five skills of disruptive leaders. New York, NY: Harper Business.

Anthony, R. (2016). The 10 characteristics of innovative leaders. Business Strategy Review, 27(3), 24-31.

## Reflection Questions

1. On a scale of 1–5, where 1 is "not at all" and 5 is "extremely", how creative and innovative am I?

   _____

   _____

   _____

   _____

   _____

2. How do I develop my creativity and innovation skills?

   _____

   _____

   _____

   _____

   _____

3. How do I foster creativity in group settings?

   _____

   _____

   _____

   _____

   _____

## Leadership

The trends in leadership in schools are changing rapidly. From K-12 to higher education, the roles of school leaders are increasingly important. With the implementation of new standards, expectations, and accountability measures, school leaders are now expected to take on a greater role in providing strategic direction, fostering collaboration, and ensuring the effective delivery of educational services. Statistics indicate that there is an increasing emphasis on collaborative leadership in schools. Leaders are now expected to lead through collaboration, dialogue, and problem-solving. This shift in leadership style is in response to the increased emphasis on school improvement and accountability. As a result, school leaders now need to be more open-minded, agile, and flexible in their approach to leading their staff and students.

While many leadership theories have evolved since one of the earliest theories—the Great Man Theory that leaders were born with innate qualities and destined to lead—to move from teacher to leader, we will focus on just two theories that align particularly well with leadership in education: Robert Greenleaf's Servant Leadership (1977) and Goleman, Boyatzis, and McKee's Six Emotional Leadership Styles (2002).

Servant leadership is a philosophy in which the leader's primary focus is on serving and empowering their team members, rather than exercising power over them to control them. Servant leadership is a type of leadership philosophy that focuses on putting the needs of those being led before the needs of the leader. This leadership style is characterized by a deep sense of humility, empathy, and a willingness to put the needs of others before one's own. This creates an environment of trust and respect, focusing on personal growth and development. A servant leader understands that true leadership is not about being in charge but about being of service to others. A servant leader takes the time to understand the needs and aspirations of their team members and works to create an environment in which each person can thrive and reach their full potential.

One of the key principles of servant leadership is to lead by example. Servant leaders are not afraid to roll up their sleeves and work alongside their team members, and they are always willing to go the extra mile to help others succeed. Servant leadership stands out as a refreshing and empowering alternative in a world where leadership is often associated with power, prestige, and control. A servant leader is someone who truly cares about the well-being of others and is committed to positively impacting the lives of those they lead.

In education, this type of leadership involves creating an environment of support and trust in which educators are empowered to reach their full potential. Servant leadership emphasizes collaboration, communication, and mutual respect in the educational setting. It is about creating a learning environment where everyone involved can contribute, be heard, and feel respected. This is the same type of environment that teachers focus on creating for their students. In this way, teachers are more likely to be engaged, motivated, and inspired to make meaningful contributions.

As a leader in education, one way to apply servant leadership is to practice active listening. You create an environment of mutual respect and understanding by actively listening to teachers, administrators, and students.

As a leader, you must also take feedback and criticism without being defensive. This allows everyone to feel valued.

Another way to apply servant leadership in education is to ensure everyone has a voice. This can include opportunities for open dialogue and allowing teachers and students to share their opinions. Creating an environment of trust and safety is important, where everyone can feel comfortable voicing their ideas and opinions. Finally, servant leadership in education requires the leader to serve as a role model. This means showing the same level of respect they expect from others and being open to feedback and criticism. By modeling the principles of servant leadership, leaders can foster an environment of trust and collaboration in which everyone is empowered to reach their potential. As a leader in education, servant leadership can be a powerful tool for creating a positive learning environment and inspiring teachers and students to reach their full potential.

Goleman, Boyatzis, and McKee's Six Emotional Leadership Styles focus on the role of emotional intelligence in leadership. As a leader in education, it is important to recognize and understand the concept of emotional intelligence (EI) and how it can apply to leadership. Popularized by psychologist and science journalist Daniel Goleman, emotional intelligence is a concept that describes the ability to identify, understand, and manage one's emotions and the emotions of others.

Goleman's model of Emotional Intelligence-Based Leadership is based on five components: self-awareness, self-regulation, motivation, empathy, and social skills.

*Self-awareness* involves understanding one's emotions, values, and strengths. Self-awareness is especially important for leaders in the education field, as it is essential for understanding how one's emotions and values affect how they interact with and lead others.

*Self-regulation* involves managing one's emotions and reactions to situations. Self-regulation is necessary when dealing with difficult situations, as it allows leaders to remain calm and respond appropriately.

*Motivation* is the ability to use emotions to guide and direct behavior in a positive direction. Motivation is key for inspiring students and staff to reach their fullest potential and work together toward a common goal.

*Empathy* is the ability to recognize, understand, and respond to the emotions of others. Empathy allows leaders to empathize with students, staff, and parents to better understand their perspectives and needs.

*Social skills* involve the ability to communicate, work, and collaborate effectively with others. By cultivating these qualities of emotional intelligence in their leadership style, leaders in education can create a successful, supportive, and engaging school environment that promotes growth and achievement.

The book *Primal Leadership* (2002) describes six different leadership styles and their effect on people's emotions. Goleman argues that leaders with high emotional intelligence are more effective at building relationships, motivating and inspiring their team members, and creating a positive work environment.

The styles are:

- **Visionary:** Inspire and motivate followers by painting a compelling picture of the future. They create a sense of purpose and direction for their followers.
- **Coaching:** Develop and mentor followers, helping them reach their full potential. They provide guidance, feedback, and support to help followers grow and develop.
- **Affiliative:** Build strong relationships and create a positive and supportive work environment. They create a sense of belonging and teamwork among their followers.
- **Democratic:** Involve followers in decision-making and create a sense of ownership and empowerment by encouraging participation and input from their followers.
- **Pacesetting:** Set high standards and lead by example, driving high performance and excellence among their followers.
- **Commanding:** Take charge and make quick, decisive decisions. They take control in crises and provide clear direction for their followers.

Each style has a different effect on the emotions of the people you're leading; also, each style works best in different situations, resonating differently with your team and producing different results. Anyone can learn how to use these leadership styles. But it's important to remember that these styles are used interchangeably, depending on the needs of your team and the situation.

## Resources

**Book:** Brown, B. (2018). Dare to lead. Vermilion.

**Book:** Folkman, J. R., & Zenger, J. H. (2019). The New Extraordinary Leader: Turning Good Managers into Great Leaders. McGraw-Hill Education.

**Book:** Goleman, D., Boyatzis, R., & McKee, A. (2002). Primal leadership: Realizing the power of emotional intelligence. Harvard Business School Press.

**Book:** Greenleaf, R. K. (1977). Servant leadership: A journey into the nature of legitimate power and greatness. Paulist Press.

**Book:** Nugent, K. (2017). 52 Weeks to Exceptional Leadership. Sojourn Publishing, LLC.

**Book:** Nugent, K. (2018). Promotion Protocol: Unlock the Secrets to Promotability and Career Success. Sojourn Publishing, LLC.

**Book:** Tree, C. (2017). Why They Buy: Cracking the Personality Code to Achieve Record Sales and Real Wealth. Aviva Publishing.

Confidence in Leadership. [Newsletter]. LinkedIn. https://www.linkedin.com/newsletters/7055727251606155264/

"How Great Leaders Inspire Action" – Simon Sinek
https://www.youtube.com/watch?v=qp0HIF3SfI4

"The Power of Vulnerability" – Brené Brown
https://www.youtube.com/watch?v=iCvmsMzlF7o

"What Makes a Great Leader" – Harvard Business Review
https://www.youtube.com/watch?v=ME5arjISTGQ

**Reflection Questions**

1. Would I identify myself as a leader? Why or why not?

_____

_____

_____

_____

_____

2. Would others consider me a leader? Why or why not?

_____

_____

_____

_____

_____

3. How can I continue to enhance my leadership skills?

_____

_____

_____

_____

_____

*Complete the sentences below:*

A leader must always…


The best leader I ever had did…


I would follow a leader who…


When I am doing a good job as a leader, I…


A leader should never…


The worst leader I had did…


I am turned off by leaders who…


Some people think they are good leaders, but they are not because…


I want to be the kind of leader who…

## Lifelong Learning

"In a world that is constantly changing, there is not one subject or set of subjects that will serve you for the foreseeable future, let alone for the rest of your life. The most important skill to acquire now is learning to learn." – John Naisbitt

With the pace of change, we must embrace lifelong learning and constantly evolve. While the concept of lifelong learning was first proposed by Basil Yeaxlee in 1929, it is more important than ever. As Peter Drucker (1959), one of the most influential management thinkers who also coined the term "knowledge worker," suggests, "We now accept the fact that learning is a lifelong process of keeping abreast of change."

The notion of *lifelong* reflects that from birth to death, we are in the process of constant learning and development that incorporates continuous professional development. Lifelong learning refers to the activities people perform throughout their life to improve their knowledge, skills, and competence in a particular field, given some personal, societal, or employment-related motives (Field, J., 2001; Aspin, D.N. & Chapman, J.D., 2000). Keep in mind that this notion reflects a range of learning activities that may range from formal activities that are intentionally planned to informal, non-intentional activities that are not planned.

Recent research has shown that having a growth mindset—the belief that intelligence can be developed—can lead to better performance and greater success in life than those with a fixed mindset, who believe that intelligence is static and cannot be changed. Lifelong learning plays a key role in developing a growth mindset. Through learning, we gain confidence in our ability to expand our intellectual and creative capacity and become more successful. By taking on new challenges and pushing ourselves to learn more, we can foster an attitude of growth and open ourselves to new ideas and perspectives.

Learning new skills and developing knowledge can also help us become more adaptive and resilient in the face of change. When we can look at a problem from different perspectives or recognize our mistakes and learn from them, we become less afraid of failure and more confident in our potential.

Lastly, lifelong learning helps us become better problem-solvers and creative thinkers. As we challenge ourselves to learn more, our brains become better wired to find solutions to difficult problems, which is essential to be a successful leader.

As you transition from teaching into a leadership role, updating certain skills and seeking learning opportunities at more advanced levels is critical. However, before you enhance your learning, it is important to assess where you are in terms of various competencies and skills. You'll find the Self-Assessment Inventory (A-Z) a useful starting point to understand where to focus your attention. Besides the areas of the Self-Assessment, there are a few other areas that are worthy to consider since you are in education.

- *Curriculum and instruction:* As an educational leader, it is helpful to be familiar with curriculum and instruction strategies that are effective within the educational setting. This includes understanding the various teaching methods and knowing which ones are best for different situations. It also includes understanding the various assessment tools available and how to properly use them.

- *Student motivation and engagement:* An educational leader must also know student motivation and engagement strategies. It is essential to understand how to create an environment where students are motivated to learn. This includes creating activities that students will be engaged in, as well as making the learning process enjoyable.
- *Educational technologies:* An educational leader must also be knowledgeable about educational technologies. This includes understanding the various software programs and devices available, as well as how to use them effectively within the classroom. It also includes understanding the different online learning options and how to maximize their use.

These are just a few of the most important things a teacher needs to learn in order to become an effective educational leader. After you've assessed your skill levels in the Self-Assessment Inventory (A-Z), it is important to understand the expectations of the educational leader role and then set specific goals to help guide the transition. Depending on your background, there are likely many new areas to continue exploring where there is a gap between your current abilities and those required in the leadership role. To develop the skills to be effective, there are several approaches that you may find helpful:

- *Seek mentorship from experienced educational leaders.* Having a mentor who can guide and advise on everything from management strategies to navigating the school system's bureaucracy can be a great way to help transition smoother.
- *Take part in professional development opportunities.* Look for professional development opportunities that can help further educate you about your new role as an educational leader. This could include conferences, webinars, or workshops.
- *Network with other educational leaders.* Establishing relationships with other educational leaders can be incredibly beneficial in helping you understand the nuances of educational leadership.
- *Stay up to date with educational trends.* Staying abreast of educational trends can help you stay on top of the latest strategies and initiatives in education.
- *Put yourself out there.* Don't be afraid to take risks and put yourself out there. Volunteering and getting involved in various initiatives is a great way to do this. It will help you gain experience and develop the skills necessary to be a successful educational leader.

Using these five strategies, teachers transitioning from the classroom to educational leadership can find the transition easier and more successful.

By continuously learning, we can expand our knowledge, become more well-rounded, more confident and adaptive, and better problem-solvers. These skills are essential for success and can lead to greater accomplishments in both our personal and professional lives.

## Resources

**Book:** Aspin, D.N., & Chapman, J.D. (2000). Lifelong learning: International perspectives on education and training. London, UK: Kogan Page.

**Book:** Brown, P. C., Roediger III, H. L., & McDaniel, M. A. (2014). Make It Stick: The Science of Successful Learning. The Belknap Press of Harvard University Press.

**Book:** Drucker, P. F. (1959). The landmarks of tomorrow. New York: Harper & Row.

**Book:** Duckworth, A. (2016). Grit: The Power of Passion and Perseverance. Scribner.

**Book:** Dweck, C. S. (2006). Mindset: The new psychology of success. Random House.

**Book:** Field, J. (2001). Lifelong learning and the new educational order. Stoke-on-Trent, UK: Trentham Books.

"Do Schools Kill Creativity?" – Sir Ken Robinson
https://www.youtube.com/watch?v=iG9CE55wbtY

"Bring on the Learning Revolution" – Sir Ken Robinson
https://www.youtube.com/watch?v=kFMZrEABdw4

"The Power of Believing You Can Improve" – Carol Dweck
https://www.youtube.com/watch?v=_X0mgOOSpLU

## Reflection Questions

1. What motivates me to learn new things?

   _____

   _____

   _____

   _____

   _____

2. How do I maintain curiosity and a desire to learn throughout my life?

   _____

   _____

   _____

   _____

3. What skills or knowledge do I feel I need to improve to become a more effective educator?

   _____

   _____

   _____

   _____

   _____

4. What strategies or resources can I use to continue my learning journey as an educator?

   _____

   _____

   _____

   _____

5. In what ways can I incorporate lifelong learning into the culture I am leading at my institution?

   _____

   _____

   _____

   _____

   _____

## Organizational Strategies

While there are many organizational strategies you will soon discover and be accountable for, there is nothing more important than focusing on the recruiting, hiring, and retention strategies of your team members.

The genie is out of the bottle, which happened during the two-and-a-half years of the pandemic. We are not going back to the ways things used to be. Innovation happened with technology online, hybrid, and new learning models.

The workforce was reevaluating their lives when they lost friends and family members to COVID. What some call the Great Resignation is when employers saw one of the most significant changes in workforce history from resignations, retirement, and rethinking.

Employees genuinely thought about what they were doing: Were they working purposefully? Was it making a difference? Was it making them happy?

Post-pandemic, our research says the workforce wants to work with purpose and know that what they do makes a difference. A newer motivating factor for younger workforce members is for the employer to provide coaching, mentoring, and training at work to mirror how they have grown up. They want career advancement opportunities, whether vertical or hierarchical. They want to be listened to and given an opportunity to provide ideas regardless of age. They want flexibility at work and in scheduling and the use of technology.

For employers, this will take innovative thinking to consider flex schedules or job sharing so you can appropriately staff while offering younger generations more flexibility to have a work-life balance. As a leader, it might require a shift in your mindset. If you do not at least consider new options and your answer is no when asked about flexibility, you might have difficulty attracting the right talent for your operation.

Every generation wants to be appreciated and recognized, which is even more true with Millennials and Generation Z. If you think your employees have a job and paycheck and that is enough, think again. Most of today's workforce is composed of Millennials and Generation Z, and they are different. To be a competitive employer, it is vital to keep up with the latest trends, or soon you will be out of business.

If you are a Baby Boomer operator or Generation X manager, you will find the workforce challenging and need new ways to adapt. If so, you may need a refresher on generations.

Today's workplace presents many challenges based solely on meeting goals, business objectives, and project deadlines. Some dynamics could present issues and conflicts throughout normal business activities if left unchecked.

Since many older workers remain on the job longer and younger workers enter the workplace right out of college, the work environment fragments into various generations. To understand this diverse environment, it is necessary to understand what generations are present in today's workplace.

A generation is a group of people born during the same period who share the same attitudes and values, world events, and technological changes. The period is the factor in dividing the generations into groups. The five generations mentioned in the next section have time ranges that define their period.

The Traditionalist Generation represents people in a generation born before 1946. The Baby Boomers are people born between 1946 and 1964. Generation X represents people born between 1965 and 1977, and Generation Y (Millennials) represents people born between 1978 and 1992. Generation Z represents people born after 1993 and 2012.

In each period are experiences that shaped the attitudes and values of each generation. In addition, the interaction between generations is also a factor in shaping the subsequent generation. For Millennials, events include the fall of the Berlin wall, Y2K, Hurricane Katrina, September 11th, the Virginia Tech shooting, Barack Obama becoming President, the Royal wedding, and same-sex marriages becoming legal (Beausoleil, 2020).

Later, the pandemic was a world event that shaped Millennials' new way of thinking. Millennials want purpose, feedback, work-life balance, and recognition (Pfau, 2016).

DeFelice (2019) writes that employers make the mistake of thinking Gen Z is just Millennials plus, but you would be wrong. One world event that shaped Gen Z was the financial crash of 2008, where their families lost jobs, retirements, etc. (DeFelice, 2019). Generation Z wants stability, consistency, and connection through face-to-face and digital interaction, craves feedback, and expects diversity, equality and inclusion, sustainability, and appreciation. According to DeFelice (2019), this generation wants flexibility and trust in their work, not necessarily in scheduling.

Because humans live an average of eighty-plus years, five potential generations may exist in the workplace today.

The five generations that exist in the workforce today are:

- Traditionalists (less than 1 percent of the workforce today)
- Baby Boomers
- Generation X
- Generation Y or Millennials (majority of the workforce today)
- Generation Z (just entering the workforce and will become the majority soon)

Given the current state of the workforce, what shifts are changing for employees? How is this different from how you see work? How are you keeping yourself on top of the trends? This is one area, as a leader, you cannot ever stop learning.

Let's now focus on why people stay in their jobs. There are four categories: social ties, purpose, pay and prospects, and inertia. According to Matthews (2022), sixteen areas are under the four categories to retain your employees. They are:

## Social Ties

- Employees want a strong, supportive manager who mentors
- Relationships with coworkers
- Leadership they trust
- Feeling included

## Purpose

- Belief in the company's mission and vision
- Satisfying and fulfilling work
- Cultural affiliation to the company
- Emotional investment in the company

## Pay and Prospects

- Fair pay
- Chance to grow and develop
- Feeling appreciated and recognized
- Clear career path

## Inertia

- Job security
- Convenience
- Nothing better elsewhere
- Golden chains

We believe this book is the key to reimagining what is possible for our workforce future in recruiting and retaining your talent while creating a sustainable mentoring program and finding new ways to learn together.

According to Gordon Food Service (2022), finding strong candidates is half the battle. So how do you do that in today's workforce and climate? "Each generation almost needs to be treated differently," says Karla Spaeth, Department Chair in Hotel, Restaurant, and Report Management at Northwood University in Michigan. The current workforce consists of Baby Boomers (born 1946–1965), Gen X (born 1966–1976), Millennials (born 1977–1992), and Gen Z (born 1993-2012).

Baby Boomers are best reached the old-fashioned way—through word of mouth, newspapers, and Facebook (Meta) or career buttons on websites. For younger generations, social network pages are best. Examples are Snagajob.com, Craigslist.com, Kijiji.com, Twitter, and Instagram, to name a few. Industry-specific sites work for faculty and staff positions.

As with every industry, educational administrators had to reinvent new recruiting strategies during and after the pandemic. With fewer people on staff, organizations are turning to technology and automation to become more agile (Schmidt, 2022).

Before you recruit, map out the ideal candidate. Create job descriptions to set expectations. Are you intentional about recruiting a diverse workforce?

Standard recruiting options are always available through LinkedIn, Indeed, Zip Recruiter, Career Builder, Monster.com, Simply Hired, Workforce Solutions, local area marketing, or trained recruiters. The problem is that every organization is using these, and you are competing for the same great next hire.

Many educational leaders are building a better candidate experience with the help of AI technology platforms such as Paradox.ai, Talroo.com, Interviewer.ai, and so many more. With multiple touchpoints, we can now keep a potential candidate engaged. Younger candidates also want mobile-friendly options to apply on their phones.

Start with networking. Identify at least ten people in your network whom you can reach out to ask for their ideas on areas to recruit and share the type of qualifications you are seeking. When mapping out the plan, include personal and professional contacts. Ask your current staff who are performing well; they may have colleagues who want the same opportunity. Staff members do not always think about the school or college like the leader. If possible, include some incentive if their contact is hired and stays at least ninety days.

Local area high schools, community colleges, career services, and university alumni groups are wonderful places to promote your job openings (Bonaparte, 2022). Professional associations related to your specific segment of education are also helpful.

Consider your local area mega-churches, which have many specific programs that may have just the right people you are looking for to fill that next position (Kolenda, 2022). Another option within local churches is the between-job ministries. This population was probably laid off and is extremely motivated to find employment while updating their resume, interviewing skills, and social image profile.

You can find opportunities when a local school closes or downsizes programs. Wordsmith your job posting to ensure it accurately describes the position and does not fall to the bottom of the site algorithm. A broader description may appeal to a candidate who wants to grow and not just do one job and, one day, have career advancement opportunities. Consider offering internships or attending job fairs.

Another place to find notable talent is through referrals from your faculty who have had great guest speakers in their class or your advisory committee members. You never know; there may be someone you connect with and they want an opportunity to become part of your mission if given a chance.

**Reflection Question**

How can I improve my recruiting practices?

_____

_____

_____

_____

## Interviewing

Hiring the right talent is the other half of the equation. Hiring success is achieved when you hire hard (Salvaggio, 2022). Prior to interviewing a candidate, much preparation has gone into the process. Many companies have found that using a behavioral-based assessment or set of behavioral-based interview questions provides a more accurate description of the candidate and transferable skills. If you have determined the traits of the ideal candidate, you can develop a set of behavioral-based questions and rating guides to provide the most objective criteria when deciding. Examples include customer service skills, honesty, integrity, work ethic, conflict management, meeting deadlines, etc. The sequencing of the questions is as follows:

- Tell me about a time when you _____.
- What action did you take?
- What were the results?
- Share with me your ideal workplace/leader/manager.
- Give me an example of when there was a problem at work or school, and you fixed it.

If your operation is not using behavioral-based techniques, search the internet for questions to get started and then develop yours based on the traits you are looking for.

According to Bizjournal.com (2018), behavioral-based interview questions provide up to an 87 percent change performance index and produce better results. Some schools and colleges often interview the candidate three times. The first can be a phone or initial interview, the second a panel interview of colleagues, and the final interview with the hiring manager. Want to know a part of their success? They hire for attitude, behavior, character, and credentials and not technical knowledge; they can train for that.

You may be so understaffed that it is tempting to make that desperate hire. Think again. One bad hire can cost the operation in terms of lower morale, decreased productivity, student retention, and loss of engagement. Promote from within when possible. It sends a strong and positive message.

## Reflection Question

How can I improve my hiring and interviewing process?

_____

_____

_____

_____

_____

## Retaining

*Orientation and Onboarding – Understanding the Differences*

Orientation is a crucial part of the onboarding experience. It introduces newly hired employees to their organization, job responsibilities, and the policies and procedures associated with the organization and their specific department. Orientation includes new employee general and departmental orientation (content and length vary by the organization).

Onboarding refers to the ongoing process of building engagement with a new employee. It starts with the acceptance of the offer letter, continues through new employee general orientation and departmental orientation, and ends when the employee becomes fully established within the organization (depending on the role, up to one year). A successful onboarding experience includes role-specific training, consistent communication, and feedback between the new employee and their manager.

With each step of the process, debriefing with leadership staff on what went well and what they can improve and documenting a continuous improvement process are imperative.

Using some type of Getting to Know You Guide or Employee Recognition Questionnaire upon hire is key. Here are some examples.

### Employee Recognition Questionnaire

This form assists leaders with their employee recognition efforts. Please complete and return the form to your manager.

1. **What are some work accomplishments or contributions you would appreciate being recognized for by your manager or supervisor?**

   Student satisfaction            Consistent job performance
   Innovative ideas or processes     Collaboration or support of team
   Taking on extra responsibilities or special projects
   Serving on a committee
   Other, please describe: _____

2. **What would you find meaningful in being recognized for the work accomplishments or contributions listed above?**

   Verbal acknowledgment         Personal note or card
   Lunch with supervisor          Administrative leave with pay
   Other, please describe: _____

3. **In what type of setting are you most comfortable receiving recognition?**

Private                                          Public

Unit/small group                           No preference

Other, please describe: _____

4. **Please list some of your favorite things so that your manager or supervisor may get to know you better. (Please fill in the blanks, if applicable.)**

Favorite drink        _____        Favorite retail store    _____

Favorite snack        _____        Favorite flower          _____

Favorite dessert      _____        Favorite sports team     _____

Favorite food         _____        Favorite restaurant      _____

Other:                _____

5. **Please provide any additional information you would like us to know.**

Another effective strategy is to conduct thirty-, sixty-, and ninety-day check-ins to ensure the employees are getting what they need to be successful.

**Check-in Questions for 30, 60, and 90 Days**

**30 Days**

1. What are your first (week's) impressions?
2. Why did you decide to accept this position?
3. On a scale of 1–10 (10 being the highest), where would you rank your enthusiasm level?
4. What do you think are some reasons we hired you?
5. What do you want to know more or less about?
6. I want you to be successful; therefore, what do you need more of or less of from me?
7. What has been your home-life conversation regarding your job? Your coworkers? What do you talk to them about?
8. What additional resources do you need?
9. What do you perceive to be your most meaningful contribution to the department in your first 30 days?
10. What have you learned about or from your coworkers? (The assumption is that the new employee has met with each department member).
11. What questions do you have for me?
12. What information are you lacking at this point that I can provide?

## 60 Days

1. Last month, you noted your enthusiasm level was ___. Has it changed, and if so, why? If it has not changed, what else is needed (to increase or to be maintained)?

2. What fuels your energy?

3. What do you want or need to know more or less about?

4. Last month, you stated you needed more or less of _____ from me.

   a. Have I followed through on that need or want?

   b. If so, how has that worked out for you? If not, what should I do differently to ensure I provide you with what you need or want?

   c. Is there anything else you need more or less of at this point?

5. Including and beyond the department, how do you feel about the working environment here?

6. Who else do you need to meet to establish rapport or relationships relative to your responsibility?

7. How do you determine your success to date in your new role?

8. What are your thoughts on the giving and receiving of feedback?

9. Do you have any questions for me?

## 90 Days

1. Where is your enthusiasm level?

2. Relative to your role/job:
   a. What keeps you up at night?
   b. What holds your interest during the day?

3. How satisfied are you with your current duties and responsibilities?

4. How do you perceive your role and contributions a year from now?

5. What does success look like a year from now, and how will you know (measure)? How will I know?

6. What can we (the department) do differently during the next year?

7. Are there things we could (need to) improve?

8. Why do you like working in this department?

9. Do you have any questions for me?

## Communication

Schedule regular staff meetings to keep everyone informed. Consider sending out a Monday morning message that recaps the week's highlights, a success story, changes in procedures, any upcoming audits, etc. The more you communicate, the better for everyone. Information is power. If you do not create your communication plan, you will have gossip running the department.

Depending on the number of staff you manage and their locations, schedule a quarterly staff meeting at a minimum. If you do not schedule them, they will not happen. Make them informative, fun, and engaging. Make the meeting worth the employee's time. Schedule one-on-one coaching sessions with each direct report at least quarterly, if not biweekly.

## Reflection Question

How can I improve my orientation and onboarding processes?

_____

_____

_____

_____

_____

## Empowering Growth and Development

Before we get started, we need working definitions. These terms are central to employees and employers, which is the next step in our retention plan.

- *Growth and development* are transformational processes in which improvement happens in your emotional, intellectual, social, and spiritual state. It reflects a commitment to developing the whole person.
- *Professional or career development opportunities* help ensure employees' knowledge and skills stay relevant and current. These opportunities allow employees to master the competencies necessary to excel in their chosen professions.
- *Bench strength* refers to an organization's ability to immediately fill critical positions with a talented internal candidate.
- *Growth mindset* (for developing talent) is a leader's attitude about their role in developing employees and their beliefs about employees' willingness and ability to grow and learn.

Did you know that providing growth and development for your team members is critical for you to keep your top talent?

Unsurprisingly, failing to deliver on this will likely be one of the strongest drivers for your high-potential employees to seek their development elsewhere.

## Research

- A survey of over 1,200 high achievers, averaging 30 years old, revealed that 95 percent engaged in regular job search activities.
- Dissatisfaction with the development available to workers featured strongly in their decision to leave the organization.
- One of the most significant factors fueling early exit was the lack of formal development.
- 70 percent of development comes from job experiences, 20 percent from learning from other people, and 10 percent through formal learning programs.

Offer a balanced menu of development opportunities to ensure you retain talent.

## Creating a Set of Options

Make a list of learning resources you are aware of that could aid your employees' growth:

| | |
|---|---|
| Your organization's resources: | |
| Education: | |
| Certifications: | |
| Books: | |
| Podcasts: | |
| Websites: | |
| Job shadowing opportunities: | |
| Cross-training: | |
| Networking/Mentoring/Buddy opportunities: | |
| Task force or committee involvement: | |
| Professional organizations (be specific): | |
| What else? | |

## Other Resources to Consider

| Personal Improvement: *Opportunities that hone a leader's skills and improve individual effectiveness* | <ul><li>Receive a 360° feedback experience.</li><li>Join the mentoring program as a protégé.</li><li>Participate in coaching.</li><li>Maintain a leadership journal.</li><li>Start a leadership reading club.</li><li>Volunteer in the community.</li><li>Volunteer for your diversity council.</li><li>Teach a course to your employees.</li><li>Join Toastmasters.</li><li>Complete Dale Carnegie.</li><li>Volunteer to lead a team effort, project, or assignment.</li><li>Volunteer to conduct a special assignment.</li><li>Participate in interim recruitment, job fairs, or college visits.</li><li>Assist junior staff in formulating their development plans.</li><li>Read at least two books every month.</li><li>Observe a leader and identify what makes that person a good leader.</li><li>Complete self-analysis instruments such as B.A.N.K., DISC, MBTI, or other style instruments.</li><li>Get feedback on results.</li><li>Join a professional association.</li><li>Attend conferences.</li><li>Subscribe to a related professional journal.</li><li>Present at a conference.</li></ul> |
|---|---|
| Open Enrollment Classes: *Sessions that may be offered internally or externally, or with podcasts, on demand* | <ul><li>Enroll in a single university course.</li><li>Identify and register for courses offered internally.</li><li>Attend an external executive education program.</li><li>Attend an internal executive education program.</li><li>Take targeted leadership classes.</li><li>Complete an advanced degree in education.</li><li>Take advantage of e-learning opportunities, such as webinars.</li><li>Listen to podcasts.</li><li>Read blogs and research wikis.</li></ul> |

| Informal or Daily Options: *Chance to experience short-term projects or processes that build skills without a great disruption in current job responsibilities* | • Take part in stretch assignments.<br>• Play an acting role when the supervisor is away.<br>• Serve as a mentor.<br>• Volunteer for an interview or hiring panel.<br>• Lead a new project.<br>• Be a "buddy" to a new employee.<br>• Work with an actively involved boss.<br>• Request on-the-job training to perfect skills. |
|---|---|
| Experiential Job Assignments: *Long- or short-term opportunities to experience diverse scenarios allow the candidate to gain organizational knowledge and prepare for broader leadership roles* | • Tour other departments or locations.<br>• Participate in an organization-wide six sigma team.<br>• Lead a cross-functional team or task force.<br>• Shadow a leader in another department.<br>• Accept a job rotation.<br>• Work at another location or department for some time.<br>• Connect with others through structured networking. |
| External Opportunities: | • Work with career field mentors from other organizations.<br>• Use sabbaticals.<br>• Be a keynote speaker at a conference.<br>• Participate in loaned executive programs.<br>• Volunteer with nonprofit organizations. |

Adapted from: ATD Creating Leadership Development Programs (Online) Certificate Program

## Reflection Question

How can I improve my growth and development opportunities for myself and my faculty and staff?

_____

_____

_____

_____

_____

## Conducting Stay Interviews

So how do you get employees to stay and love it in your organization? Show them you care (Kaye & Jordan-Evans, 2008*).*

A stay interview is a positive, scheduled, structured, informal discussion a leader conducts with an individual employee to identify specific actions the leader can take to strengthen the employee's engagement and increase their likelihood of staying with the organization.

A stay interview is not a performance discussion.

Leaders will conduct one stay interview per employee each calendar year.

Do you know the top reasons employees quit their jobs? Why wait until they leave to find out? Become proactive and use stay interviews annually. Do you know the cost of losing one employee? It goes beyond the financial costs, such as lower employee morale, loss of operational experience, more overtime paid, burnout on other staff, etc.

Three primary skills go into an effective stay interview: listening, note-taking, and probing questions.

- Listening is critical. Avoid distractions such as your cell phone, computer, etc.

- The interview is your time to be *fully attentive* to the employee and what they are saying. Use open and positive body language and smile. Do not interrupt!

- Taking notes creates a record of this critical conversation for reference when you cocreate the stay plan and show the employee their feedback matters.

- Probing is your ability to ask open-ended questions without commenting on what they say.

- Do not feel the need to answer questions or solve problems during the stay interview.

A stay interview is a scheduled twenty- to thirty-minute meeting with an employee one-on-one. Put your phone away and avoid distractions. You can gather sample questions from the internet. Some of my favorite questions are:

- On your drive to work each morning, what are you thinking about? What are you excited about as you come to work each day?

- What skills and talents would you like to contribute every day?

- How are we fully utilizing your skills and talents in your role?

- What job factors are you passionate about?

- If you could learn one additional topic related to your job, what would it be?

- What kind of feedback is most helpful to you?

- How do you decide when it is safe to talk to a supervisor or coworker about something difficult?

The stay interview is a positive reset for you and the employee to reengage and for you to learn from them and listen.

## Reflection Question

How can I improve employee engagement?

_____

_____

_____

_____

_____

## Creating a Culture of Recognition

Did you ever think you could start a recognition program from day one? Here are some ideas to get you started. Employees consistently rank recognition in the five stay factors within an organization. No one leaves an organization because they feel over-appreciated, but the opposite is true. Do you ever hear your employees say how much they love what they do or how much they feel appreciated? Here are some ideas on what you can do:

### Day One Recognition

- Offer to be an onboarding "buddy" for new employees.
- Have a welcome poster signed by the team on the first day.
- Do a first-day e-card from the manager and colleagues.
- Ensure the new employee's workstation has all the tools and access.
- Introduce the new employee to everyone in the department.
- Take them to lunch.
- Ask how the job is going and offer to help!

### Additional Ideas for Recognition

- Recognition photo display in break areas.
- Off-site team building.
- Use team meetings or huddles to recognize milestones and achievements.
- Candy bar with a special note.
- Written email or framed certificate from the leadership team for meeting goals.
- Start the meeting out with a fun quote or quick YouTube video or music to change the energy—put thought into your meetings so they see you care.
- Lunch and Learns.
- Virtual get-togethers.
- End-of-year banquet or awards.
- Send a thank-you letter once a candidate accepts your offer letter.
- Recognition in front of peers.
- Send birthday, anniversary, and special-event e-cards.
- Handwritten notes.
- Surprise the employee with a special treat or book such as "You are a lifesaver" and a roll of Life Savers.
- Make your virtual meetings fun.

- Host food days to celebrate.
- Celebrate national days or national weeks.
- Employee competition.
- Cookies delivered to the house.
- Traveling trophy.
- Virtual bulletin board posting team achievements.
- Pay-it-forward program.
- Posting praise from a customer.
- Have peers call out cheers for each other for accomplishments.
- Ask your employees what they would like.
- Track the team's wins.
- Feature employee of the month.
- Create a virtual wall of fame.
- Give rewards that are career based, such as sending an employee to a leadership class or training or certification class.
- Encourage mentoring, virtual or otherwise.
- Create a virtual suggestion box.
- Say "Thank you".

## Reflection Question

How am I building a culture of recognition?

_____

_____

_____

_____

_____

## Reimagine the Future

The latest trends and research show significant generational differences in our workforce from Generation Z to Baby Boomers. While it is easy to share the trends, operationally adjusting is the challenge. It is up to you to adjust to recognize and adopt alternative approaches for each generation in your organization. Conflict often arises due to negative assumptions and a lack of knowledge. The younger generations see a mismatch between what they think a business should try to achieve and actual priorities (Pulver, 2021). Do you wonder why? Look at what they have seen while growing up from the Enron scandal, Bernie Madoff, and so much more. No wonder we turn them off!

It is crucial for the younger generation to see the purpose—what you do matters, great company culture, professional development opportunities to work and grow, and work-life balance (flexibility in scheduling). Of course, the manager and team members are key to creating a sense of belonging.

We might underestimate that they are free to leave when they do not think the workplace is fair. Think back to when you were nineteen or twenty-five; maybe you felt the same way and have forgotten now that you have experienced and learned so much in your career. They need you more than ever!

If you are an influential leader, your employees will thrive. If not, reassess your leadership traits and see how you can shift.

If this happens to you, you need to know why your employees are leaving, so do not wait for the exit interview. Use the strategies shared so far. Long gone are the days of one size fits all.

## Reflection Question

How can I improve your knowledge of generational differences and adjust my style?

_____

_____

_____

_____

_____

## Gap Analysis for the Leader to Complete

Are you the problem or the solution?

| Operational Questions | On a scale of 1 to 10, with 1 being poor and 10 being best in class | Action steps needed to close the gap |
|---|---|---|
| Are your mission, vision, and value statements memorable? | | |
| Have you created the ideal candidate profiles? | | |
| Are your job descriptions documented? | | |
| Have you clearly defined expectations? | | |
| Do you have a comprehensive hiring strategy? | | |
| Are your salaries competitive? Do you have fair hourly rates? | | |
| Do you have a strong benefits package? | | |
| Do you allow employees to take part in interview panels? | | |
| Do you have a pipeline of candidates/bench strength? | | |

| | | |
|---|---|---|
| Do you understand what is important to each generation and change accordingly? | | |
| Do you use behavioral-based interview questions/assessments? | | |
| Do you have a formal orientation and welcoming process? | | |
| Do you use an employee recognition questionnaire to determine what is important to the employee? | | |
| Do you have an effective yearlong onboarding program? | | |
| Do you assign a buddy for the first 90 days? | | |
| Do you conduct 30-, 60-, and 90-day check-ins? | | |
| Do you have an effective and consistent communication plan? | | |
| Do you provide education or certification financial support? | | |
| Do you ask employees for their ideas? | | |
| Do you have an official mentoring program in place? | | |

| | | |
|---|---|---|
| Is job shadowing offered? | | |
| Are there advancement opportunities—career lattices/ladders? | | |
| Do you offer flexible scheduling options? | | |
| Do you conduct stay interviews annually, at a minimum? | | |
| Do you perform performance evaluations (quarterly or annually)? | | |
| Are you addressing reskilling to build new career pathways? | | |
| Do you have an effective and accessible recognition program? | | |
| Do you provide ongoing feedback? | | |
| Do employees know they can talk to you? | | |
| Have you created a culture of psychological safety? | | |
| Do you offer upskilling opportunities to meet the demands of the future? | | |

| | | |
|---|---|---|
| Do you schedule one-on-one coaching meetings? | | |
| Do you facilitate effective staff meetings? | | |
| Do you have fun at work? | | |
| Have you created a company retention plan and assess it quarterly? | | |

| Personal Leadership Self-Assessment Questions | On a scale of 1 to 10, with 1 being poor and 10 being best in class | Action steps needed to close the gap |
|---|---|---|
| As the leader, are you investing in yourself? | | |
| Are you a mentor manager? | | |
| Are you staying out front and analyzing trends on the cutting edge? | | |
| How comfortable are you with addressing conflict effectively? | | |
| Are you a leader your employees want to follow regardless of location? | | |
| Can you delegate effectively to empower and grow your team members? | | |
| Do you know yourself and your talents? | | |
| How do you stay healthy? | | |
| As a leader, how do you keep yourself from getting discouraged? | | |
| How do you stay abreast of new technology? | | |

## Project Management

As a leader in education, it is important to understand the fundamentals of project management to effectively lead and manage projects. Project management is a crucial approach to increasing the productivity of organizations and improving internal operations, responding to opportunities, and achieving strategic goals. Some people perceive that education is so unique and context-specific, given the pressures for decentralization and competitiveness, that project management cannot be used. However, I've had the privilege of developing project management programs both at the undergraduate and graduate level, serving as a project manager on countless projects and working with several schools where I had a project manager to assist me. I've seen that knowledge of these powerful skills and the proper application of project management techniques is very effective.

*Project management* is planning, organizing, motivating, and controlling resources to achieve specific goals. It is the application of knowledge, skills, tools, and techniques to project activities to meet the project requirements. Project management can address a wide variety of challenges in education. For example, it can help leaders in education identify issues, develop solutions, and ensure projects are delivered on time, with the quality desired and within budget. It can also ensure that everyone involved in the project clearly understands the goals, roles, and expectations. In project management, leaders in education can use various tools and techniques, such as project charters, project plans, risk management, resource management, and communication plans to plan, organize, and control projects.

A *project charter* is a document that outlines the objectives, scope, and deliverables for the project, along with the roles and responsibilities of each team member. A project should always have a clearly defined goal. It is important to ensure that everyone involved in the project is aware of their responsibilities, the timeline of the project, and the expected outcome. A timeline outlining the steps and activities needed to achieve the project objectives should be created. This will help keep the project moving forward and ensure everyone knows the expected timeline.

*Project plans* are used to track progress against goals, objectives, and tasks. It is important to monitor progress to ensure the project is on track and meeting expected goals.

*Risk management* is used to identify and manage risks associated with the project.

*Resource management* is used to ensure that the right people, equipment, and materials are available when needed.

A *budget* should ensure that the project is managed within the resources. This will also help ensure that any additional costs are properly accounted for. *Communication plans* are used to ensure that everyone understands the project goals, tasks, and expectations. As a leader, one must communicate regularly with all stakeholders to ensure that the project continues moving forward and any issues are addressed promptly. Project management also helps leaders in education ensure that projects are completed on time, within budget, and with quality. Through project management, leaders can identify potential risks and develop mitigation strategies. They can also make certain that tasks are properly delegated and that communication is clear. Project management also helps leaders monitor progress and adjust plans as needed. By understanding the fundamentals of project management, leaders in education can more effectively lead their teams and ensure that their projects are successful.

Project management is a complex process that requires a thorough understanding of the principles and practices of successful project management to ensure successful completion of goals. According to the PMBOK (Project Management Body of Knowledge), there are five steps in project management that are central to achieving project success:

1. *Initiating*: This first step involves developing a comprehensive project plan that outlines all the activities that need to be done, the resources needed, and the timeline for completion. It is important to identify the project, allocate resources, and set objectives in this stage. Also, it is helpful to identify the key stakeholders—the range of individuals, including potential partners, decision-makers, and sponsors with a vested interest in the issue or project.

2. *Planning*: Once the project is established, the project manager must create a detailed plan that includes identifying risk, setting up team roles and responsibilities, defining budget and timelines, and creating a project schedule.

3. *Executing*: This is the stage where the project management team implements the plan. It involves managing resources, overseeing and coordinating activities, communicating with stakeholders, and making sure that the project is completed within the agreed-upon time frame and budget.

4. *Monitoring and controlling:* This is the stage where the project manager tracks the project's progress and makes adjustments when necessary. It also involves tracking costs, monitoring the team's performance, and providing feedback to stakeholders to ensure the project is on track.

5. *Closing*: The last step in the project management process involves completing and evaluating the project's success. This includes analyzing the team's performance, delivering the final project results, and archiving project documents. By understanding and following the steps outlined in the PMBOK, whether you're a leader in education or the actual project manager, you can help ensure the successful completion of the projects.

## Resources

**Book:** Kerzner, H. R. (2006). Project Management for Education: The Bridge to 21st Century Learning. John Wiley & Sons.

**Book:** Project Management Institute. (2017). A Guide to the Project Management Body of Knowledge (PMBOK Guide). Project Management Institute.

"Intro to Project Management Certificate" (and other videos): https://www.youtube.com/watch?v=rck3MnC7OXA

"Project Structures & Lifecycles" https://www.youtube.com/watch?v=8unOyycCpFs

## Reflection Questions

1. What are my strengths and weaknesses as a project manager?

_____

_____

_____

_____

_____

2. How can I build on my strengths and address my weaknesses?

_____

_____

_____

_____

_____

3. How can I effectively communicate with stakeholders, including teachers, administrators, and students, throughout the project management process?

_____

_____

_____

_____

4. How can I balance competing priorities, such as budget constraints, project timelines, and quality assurance, to ensure project success?

_____

_____

_____

_____

5. How can I foster a culture of collaboration and teamwork among project team members and leverage their strengths and expertise to achieve project goals?

_____

_____

_____

_____

## Strategic Planning

As an education leader, strategic planning is a critical component of your success. Strategic planning is determining a vision and mission, setting goals, and developing strategies to achieve those goals. It is an ongoing process that involves setting goals, analyzing data, and taking action to ensure the best possible outcomes for your students, staff, and community.

When it comes to strategic planning, it is important to clearly understand the status of the school and the desired future state. A strategic plan is like a road map, almost like creating a travel route from where you are to where you want to go (from point A to point B). There are many ways you can get there. However, the plan will help guide you once you know the destination. It is important for education leaders to understand the strategic planning process to ensure that their organization is on the right path.

Analogies between sport and business are very common, and in business, we use a lot of sporting terminology like, "Let's make sure we don't drop the ball on this one," and "Remember, it's a marathon, not a sprint." And in both sports and business, our goal is to beat the competition, and that is what strategy is all about—finding the unique way your company can garner a sustainable competitive advantage.

In sports, however, the strategy is relatively simple—get more points than your opponent—and implementation is also relatively straightforward. Train hard and practice hard. If you are fitter, have better skills, and if it's a team sport, you coordinate your efforts better than the competition and have a better chance of winning.

In business, it's not quite that simple. There are many people with exceptional skills, who work very hard, but still see their businesses fail. A coherent strategic plan gives the school a target, a vision of what it can be at its best. And then begins the hard work of coordinating and aligning all available resources to make that vision reality.

The strategic planning process typically begins with a review of the organization's mission and vision. This is an important step as it helps ensure the organization is aligned with its goals and objectives. It is also important to assess the current state of your school. From there, the organization can develop a set of goals that are aligned with its mission and vision. These goals should address factors such as resources, personnel, and technology. It is also important for education leaders to understand the resources and how to best use them to reach the desired goals. These goals should also be specific, measurable, attainable, relevant, and time-based (SMART).

Consider any areas of improvement that need to be addressed, and then set SMART goals. Then, create a plan of action that outlines how you will meet those goals and how you will measure progress and success. Next, collect and analyze data to better understand your school. Look at student performance, teacher turnover rates, and other important metrics. This data will inform your strategy and help you set realistic goals.

Once your goals are set and your data is collected, it's time to create a timeline for implementation. Identify and prioritize the actions that need to be taken and then develop and assign tasks to ensure the plan is laid out clearly and efficiently. Finally, implement the plan and measure its success. Evaluate the data collected, analyze the results, and adjust the plan where needed. Strategic planning is an ongoing process, so continue to monitor and adjust your plan as needed. By following these steps and taking a strategic approach to planning, you can ensure that your school will have the best possible outcomes. Before you know it, you will be on your way to success.

In 1996 Michael Porter wrote his much-heralded article for the *Harvard Business Review* entitled "What is Strategy?" which became a classic for subsequent students of business strategy. Porter argued that operational effectiveness, which means improving efficiency by, for example, incorporating best practices or the latest technology, is a necessary but in*sufficient* condition for an organization's success. As a company develops operational efficiency—such as better internal systems or a better distribution channel—it certainly gains an edge in the market, but only temporarily. Pretty soon, the competition can copy that efficiency, which, at the industry level, makes the whole industry more efficient but, at the company level, destroys any advantage one company may have had over another.

Success for the company, Porter said, was all about developing *and maintaining* a unique competitive advantage. So operational efficiency might be critical to a company's long-term success, but it isn't *strategy.* Strategy, Porter said, involves choosing a unique set of activities that can be combined in such a way that your company can offer a superior value proposition to the market. Only by determining what your company can do better than any other company can you find a real competitive advantage. And, even then, it will not last.

Over the long term, almost anything can be replicated. If an organization does not take the time and effort to develop a competitive strategy, then by default its strategy is, "We will create no domains of excellence." That path will doom the company to mediocrity and, eventually, extinction. But determining what competitive advantages the company has and what further advantages it needs to develop is just the first step.

Next, Porter said, the company has to consider trade-offs. Resources are always limited, and no firm can excel in every aspect of their product or service. Therefore, there must be tradeoffs based on what the company can do best, what the competition offers, and what criteria matter most to the customers they strive to serve. The company must clearly define those few things at which it can be world-class, and whatever is not essential to that goal must be jettisoned. Developing a strategy is more about saying no than saying yes.

The third step, Porter says, is applying the concept of "fit." Fit refers to aligning the company's internal and external activities to support each other to achieve the company's strategic intent. The aim here is symbiosis—everything working together. So, as we consider the appropriateness of our strategy, we determine the unique set of qualities that deliver our competitive advantage. Then we make the trade-offs to ensure we're not wasting resources doing anything else. We check that everything we do to manage and operate the company fits—that it aligns with our strategic goal. That is part of the equation, as there are always environmental challenges because of the economy, the marketplace, customers, and technology. None of it ever stops moving, meaning strategy must flex and adapt. During the past several years, we witnessed this as the COVID-19 pandemic affected everyone, and education was often forced into a new modality of learning with online and other approaches.

Sometimes it is even necessary to recognize that a strategy is no longer viable and must be rethought from the ground up.

So, to develop a strategic plan as a leader, you must answer the following questions:

- What do we want to ultimately accomplish? What is our vision?
- What is our organization about? What is our mission?
- How do we want to accomplish our goals? What are our values?

And with a school, there may be more granular questions worth asking that will help shape some fundamental choices around the operating model:

- What customer segments or *target audience* should we focus on?
- How do we create sustainable differentiation with a unique *value proposition*?
- How do we drive down *student acquisition costs*?
- What is the right *program mix* and *educational approach*?
- How do we decrease *the cost of serving* our students?
- How do we speed up *growth*?

By answering these questions, a strategic plan can help guide decision-making, innovation, and responsiveness. It also can help increase engagement and align the school, so the odds of the execution of the plan increase dramatically.

## Resources

**Book:** Chan Kim, W., & Mauborgne, R. (2005). Blue Ocean Strategy: How to Create Uncontested Market Space and Make the Competition Irrelevant. Harvard Business Review Press.

**Book:** Porter, M.E. (1998) Competitive Strategy: Techniques for Analyzing Industries and Competitors. Free Press.

**Book:** Rumelt, R. (2011). Good Strategy/Bad Strategy: The Difference and Why It Matters. Currency.

**Book:** Stavros, J.M., & Hinrichs, G. 2009. The Thin Book of SOAR: Building Strengths-Based Strategy. Thin Book Publishing Co.

"A Plan Is Not a Strategy" – Harvard Business Review https://www.youtube.com/watch?v=iuYlGRnC7J8

"Changing Paradigms" – Sir Ken Robinson https://www.youtube.com/watch?v=mCbdS4hSa0s

**Reflection Questions**

1.  What are my organization's long-term goals, and how can I align my strategies to achieve those goals?

    _____

    _____

    _____

    _____

    _____

2.  What are my organization's unique strengths and weaknesses, and how can I leverage or mitigate them in my strategies?

    _____

    _____

    _____

    _____

    _____

3.  What are the potential risks and uncertainties in my strategies, and how can I prepare for and manage them?

    _____

    _____

    _____

    _____

    _____

4.  How can I build a culture of innovation and continuous improvement in my organization, and how can I adapt to changes in the external environment?

    _____

    _____

    _____

    _____

    _____

5.  How can I engage and empower your team members to contribute to the development and implementation of my strategies?

_____

_____

_____

_____

_____

## Identifying Opportunities and Threats

The following fifteen questions will help your institution identify opportunities and threats.

What quantitative "evidence" could you collect and analyze to provide answers to the questions?

| | Yes | No |
|---|---|---|
| 1. Are there additional potential student segments we could serve?<br>Evidence: | | |
| 2. Could we diversify our program offerings in our areas of expertise to gain strength?<br>Evidence: | | |
| 3. Are regulatory requirements increasing?<br>Evidence: | | |
| 4. Are we at risk regarding any regulatory requirements?<br>Evidence: | | |
| Have the demographics of our student body changed?<br>Evidence: | | |
| 6. Are our students' needs and/or expectations changing?<br>Evidence: | | |

| | | |
|---|---|---|
| 7. Do other schools that attract our students have an advantage?<br>Evidence: | | |
| 8. Are there local or state economic changes that impact our institution?<br>Evidence: | | |
| 9. Could we gain better control or quality in our relationships with suppliers of goods and services to our institution?<br>Evidence: | | |
| 10. Are we up to date and informed by current research and practice models of student retention?<br>Evidence: | | |
| 11. Do we use quantitative measures to benchmark and assess our progression toward our retention goals?<br>Evidence: | | |
| 12. Do we offer programs to help students with the financial and student success skills they need?<br>Evidence: | | |

| | | |
|---|---|---|
| 13. Do we have a strong default prevention and debt management plan?<br>Evidence: | | |
| 14. Does each member of the staff and faculty understand their role in and responsibilities regarding student retention?<br>Evidence: | | |
| 15. Are our retention goals reasonable and attainable?<br>Evidence: | | |

## Teamwork

As you move into a leadership role in education, you'll quickly discover that getting people to work together isn't always easy. I've heard many leaders comment specifically that getting teachers to work together is like herding cats. However, it doesn't have to be that way, especially if you have the right approach during the first few weeks and months in a leadership role. There are steps you can take to create a team that is more likely to be successful. There are other basic things that many leaders skip over as they jump right into focusing on goals.

Rather than making the mistake of focusing on tasks and goals right away, one of your very first priorities needs to be getting to know everyone on the team while helping them get to know each other even better. Building strong relationships and having that focus initially is critical. This is an area where you can leverage the powerful B.A.N.K. personality system discussed in the section on communication. As a reminder, this tool is a game changer when it comes to helping people develop emotional intelligence, which is an essential part of a high-performing team.

To get your complimentary report in less than 90 seconds, please visit: www.crackmycode.com/learn

To get a custom link for your organization, contact Dr. Eric Goodman at: eric@higheredchange.com

The information in this report provides insight into each individual's strengths and how best to communicate with them. It also provides insights into understanding how the person will behave under stress. When shared across a team, this information allows people to be more fully engaged since they are valued and appreciated for who they are and the talents they bring to the team. If they are treated as a cog in the wheel or as a thing, they will not be fully engaged or committed to the work. By deepening this understanding of each person, you will learn what they value and how best to provide a motivating environment for them. It will also help avoid conflicts and allow you to leverage each person based on their underlying values. After all, every team has certain roles that need to be fulfilled, and you need to ensure that you have the right people on the team and they are in the right roles. This is an important thing to assess for everyone you lead. Simply asking whether you would hire that person again and whether that person is in the right position is a great starting point. There are several other helpful questions you could ask, like:

1. How is the team currently performing?
2. Does the team lack any critical skills to be able to achieve excellence? And if so, what are they?
3. How do the strengths of the team and each individual complement each other?
4. How best can I support the development of each person? What are their aspirations?
5. What unique contribution can each person make to add the most value to the team while leveraging their passion, skills, and expertise?

As you get to know each person and the team, another key is establishing group norms and setting expectations and goals while creating an environment where everyone feels comfortable (i.e., think psychological safety) and motivated to contribute. Everyone must understand their roles and responsibilities and how they can contribute to the team's success. It is imperative to set clear expectations and provide the necessary resources to ensure everyone is on the same page.

As an academic leader, one of the most important responsibilities is cultivating a diverse team. A diverse team of individuals can bring a variety of experiences, perspectives, and ideas to the table, which can help to foster creativity, innovation, and problem-solving in any workplace. Building and managing a team from different backgrounds can be challenging, but it is an essential part of creating a positive and productive environment.

Here are several tips to help you create and maintain a diverse team:

- *Develop a culture of belonging.* Make sure that everyone in your team feels welcome and valued. Create an open and welcoming environment where everyone is encouraged to share their ideas and perspectives. Unfortunately, many diversity, equity, and inclusion efforts haven't achieved the desired results. It seems they don't go far enough to truly create a culture of belonging, which is more of a mental and emotional state of being seen, valued, and supported based on one's uniqueness. When you look at the lack of engagement and Great Resignation based on studies by organizations like the Gallup Institute and McKinsey & Co, it is easy to recognize that the lack of belonging may be one of the top drivers negatively impacting the workforce. To counteract this, you may also utilize employee resource groups or affinity groups to provide a safe space for those from marginalized or underrepresented backgrounds to communicate and build a stronger sense of belonging and community.

- *Prioritize diversity in hiring.* When hiring people, strive to create a team with a wide range of backgrounds and experiences. As you build your team, keep an open mind and ensure that all perspectives are represented. Encourage your team to bring their life experiences, perspectives, and ideas to the table. Pay attention to the demographics of your team and ensure that it is representative of the diversity of your student body and community.

- *Foster collaboration.* Encourage team members to work together and collaborate on projects. This can help reduce tension and create an atmosphere of respect and inclusion.

- *Provide resources.* Make sure that faculty, staff, and students have the resources they need to be successful. Provide them with training, mentorship, and support to help them develop their skills and abilities. Building and managing a diverse team can be a challenge, but it is an essential part of creating a positive and productive environment. By developing a culture of inclusion, prioritizing diversity in hiring, fostering collaboration, and providing resources, you can create a team that is truly representative of the diversity of your student body and community.

- *Focus on results.* A team is only as strong as its weakest link. When delegating tasks, consider each team member's strengths and weaknesses, and assign tasks accordingly. Measure progress and provide feedback to help everyone reach their potential. By following these tips, you can create and manage a diverse team working together toward a common goal. With a little effort and commitment, you can ensure the team is successful, productive, and ultimately happy.

- *Create accountability.* Finally, it is important to hold yourself and your team accountable. Create an inclusive work environment by setting clear expectations and providing consistent feedback. Additionally, create opportunities for development and growth, such as mentorship programs or professional development courses. By taking these steps, you can create and manage a productive, engaged, and empowered team.

## Resources

**Book**: Coyle, D. (2018). The Culture Code: The Secrets of Highly Successful Groups. Bantam.

**Book:** Dyer, W.G. Jr., Dyer, J.H. and Dyer, W.G. (2013). Team Building: Proven Strategies for Improving Team Performance. Jossey-Bass.

**Book:** Patterson, K., Grenny J., McMillan, R. and Switzler, A. (2011)
Crucial Conversations: Tools for Talking When Stakes Are High. McGraw-Hill Education

"Are You an Ideal Team Player?" – Patrick Lencioni https://www.youtube.com/watch?v=PRh80RyT74I

"Trusting Teams – The 5 Practices" – Simon Sinek https://www.youtube.com/watch?v=W5qQJhe7sLE

## Reflection Questions

1.  How do I ensure that all team members have a clear understanding of their roles and responsibilities?

    _____

    _____

    _____

    _____

    _____

2.  How do I build trust and respect among team members?

    _____

    _____

    _____

    _____

    _____

3.  What are some of the challenges I have faced when building teams in the past?

    _____

    _____

    _____

    _____

    _____

4.  What steps can I take to ensure team members feel valued and supported?

    _____

    _____

    _____

    _____

    _____

5.  How do I promote a culture of collaboration and continuous improvement within the team?

    _____

    _____

    _____

    _____

    _____

## Time Management

The more effective your time management skills, the more effective leader you will become. Many people get distracted throughout the day or do not have a structure to capture top-priority items. Before we can discuss time management, reflect on where you waste time. If you are unsure, keep a weekly time log, writing about how you spend each waking hour. This will give you some insight into what to change.

It is vital to start your day with a healthy morning routine. Be intentional. Listen to something motivating when you first get up. Missy Day (2023) suggests asking yourself the following questions:

- What is the most time-sensitive project I am working on?
- What is the biggest contribution I can make to my team and company right now?
- What task will cause other people chaos if it does not get done today?
- Which strategic tasks will help me work smarter tomorrow?

What structure do you use to keep your appointments in front of you? If you are not currently using a digital calendar, capture all your commitments. Use one calendar and not two calendars. Place all personal and professional commitments on your calendar. If the calendar is provided by your employer, it is possible to use the private icon for personal commitments. The danger in using two calendars is something will be dropped off, or you can be double-booked without realizing it. Make sure your calendar is visible on your phone as well.

The next step in the process is to create a to-do list. We suggest using a digital capturing system rather than paper and rewriting your to-do list on paper every day, which wastes time. It is far better to delete tasks when accomplished by simply deleting the tasks in one step electronically. We can easily add new tasks throughout the day.

Once you have created this list, focusing on the top priority items is essential. Some people like using the Eisenhower Matrix to prioritize their to-do list. It is a four-square framework of urgent, not urgent, important, and not important. From there, you decide to do, schedule, delegate, or delete. Other people enjoy using Stephen Covey's four-square matrix of:

- Quadrant 1: Urgent and important
- Quadrant 2: Not urgent and yet important
- Quadrant 3: Urgent but not important
- Quadrant 4: Not urgent and not important

For even more strategies, check out *The 7 Habits of Highly Successful People.*

This will take practice, but the more you use these strategies, the more muscle memory you'll build. The more you accomplish, the more engaged and energetic you will feel.

Avoid multitasking. It may appear you can do many things all at once. However, you will not do them well, nor will you be present. When you have scheduled meetings with your team members, put your phone away and do not look at your computer or emails. Make sure you start and end your appointments on time. Your team will thank you.

Once you complete your work for the week, before going home, review the next week's calendar day by day. What needs to be done today before you leave so you can enjoy the weekend? Have you set up an agenda for any meetings you have set? Are there any reports you are accountable for next week? Are you speaking at an event, and have you written your speech? These are just some examples. Once you complete this, it is time to go home, have fun, and be present! You will be so glad you have this system in place, and so will your family.

**Reflection Questions**

1. What system do I use for time management?

_____

_____

_____

_____

_____

2. How do I focus on high-priority items?

_____

_____

_____

_____

_____

3. Do I use one calendar for professional and personal tasks?

_____

_____

_____

_____

_____

# MENTORSHIP

**Mentor Self-Assessment – Are You Ready to Be a Mentor Manager?**

Good leadership requires empathy, which is your ability to connect and relate to your employees. According to Clint Pulver (2021), a mentor manager is "where the magic happens!" (p.64–65). There are high expectations and a high connection with employees. According to Pulver, employees give their mentor manager respect and loyalty and engage with their work and coworkers. The mentor looks for the employees' potential while building trust and asking questions along the way. So how do you do that?

Using the second half of this book will provide you with a structured way to build trust, empathy, kindness, connection, and care.

The purpose of mentoring is to provide the leaders, department directors, supervisors, and peers with a structured roadmap. You will draw from personal career experience and professional excellence. Feedback and coaching skills are secondary.

1. What is your why or purpose for being a mentor?
2. Conduct a SOAR analysis as a mentor manager of yourself:

    - My strengths are _____.
    - My opportunities are _____.
    - My aspirations are _____.
    - The results I want to achieve are _____.

3. Motivation

    - What is motivating you to take on mentoring?
    - Do you have the confidence and competence to be a mentor?
    - What is your vision of the best possible outcome?
    - Do you feel you can make a connection and build trust?
    - What obstacles might prevent you from reaching the mentee's goals?

4. List the action steps for how you will:

   - Communicate
   - Use your personal experience
   - Adapt resources to the mentee's learning style
   - Deal with resistance
   - Be involved

5. What are the new skills, knowledge, and attitudes needed to make this change?

   - Skills
   - Knowledge
   - Attitudes

6. Determine how you will acknowledge, recognize, and celebrate after the program.
7. How will you keep the momentum?
8. Goal setting:

   - What are the mentee's career goals?
   - What is the mentee's motivation for life?

9. Initial conversation starters:

   - How is it going?
   - What did you accomplish this week?
   - What did you learn about yourself this week?
   - Catch me up.

Getting to know your mentee is essential for this relationship to work.

## Communication Strategies

- Build connections and trust.
- Be empathetic.
- Use active listening.
- Explore options; there is plenty of time.
- Provide encouragement.

- Cocreate opportunities.
- Acknowledge the effort they are putting in.

## Facilitating/Asking Questions

The remarkable thing about this book is that we have created the questions for you. You can certainly expand on them. We want to caution you about what is not helpful regarding the approach. We have found that these approaches are not useful in the mentoring relationship. Remember:

- You are not a therapist.
- Be a friend first before being a mentor. Developing a strong bond of trust is critical.
- Telling them everything you have done for the past twenty to forty years is not the focus.
- Asking questions is most helpful in this relationship. Sometimes, mentees are looking for answers, and that is when your experience can help guide them.
- Do not push your agenda.
- Do not solve their problems. The mentee needs to solve the problem for themselves. If there is a week when you feel the mentee is going in the wrong direction, pause the conversation. Ask the mentee to write their thoughts and what they want to accomplish and pick it up next week. You both need time to reflect. Do not push it if it does not feel right.
- Do not tell them what to do.

## Feedback

- Do not ask "why" questions. It puts people on the defensive, and behaviors do not change. Once a relationship is established, your questions will come naturally.
- Begin discussions with "how" or "what" questions.
- Always be respectful of your mentee.
- Actively listen to what they say.

## Problem-Solving

Use this model to problem solve (Connellan, 2002):

- Define the issue.
- Explore options.
- Develop solutions.
- Reinforce positive ideas.
- Close the deal/gain agreements. Do not assume anything; ask for their commitment.

## Reflection on Learning

- How are you doing?
- What is working?
- Where are you struggling, or what are you confused about?

## Structure

- Commit to meet once a week. Be flexible.
- Use phone, face-to-face, or web-based technology if allowed.
- Set the time and date.
- Take notes.
- Mentor relationships can be one-on-one, or a mentor can actively mentor small groups of up to four people.

## Celebrate Learning/Rewards

- Utilize thank-you notes.
- Provide face-to-face acknowledgment.

The research is clear that having a mentor in life is immensely helpful. While many organizations start mentoring programs, the programs rarely produce the intended result or merely do not remain active. To prevent this from happening, preparation is key.

## Preparation and Expectations for the Mentor

- Review and commit to the schedule.
- Read the chapter or article for the week.
- Review the self-assessment questions.
- Review the mentor questions.
- Think about how you can expand the conversation based on the goals and your experience. Feel free to bring in additional resources.

*"People will forget what you said, people will forget what you did, but people will never forget how you made them feel."*

– Maya Angelou

# HERE IS AN EXAMPLE OF A MENTOR/MENTEE AGREEMENT THAT CAN BE USED THAT OUTLINES A STRUCTURED PATH TO DEVELOP LEADERSHIP SKILLS

We are both excited about embarking on this journey together. We both want this to be a rewarding experience, spending most of our time discussing developmental activities that will provide valuable knowledge in the future. We agree that:

1. The mentoring relationship will last for a minimum of six months. If, for some reason, it does not meet the needs of the mentee, we can decide to end the formal relationship at any time through a conversation.

2. We will meet weekly via face-to-face, phone, or Zoom. Meeting times, once agreed, should not be canceled unless this is unavoidable. At the end of each meeting, we will agree on a date for the next meeting.

3. Each meeting can range from 30 to 60 minutes, but the mentor and mentee should choose what is best for both parties. (Free Zoom allows up to 40 minutes.)

4. We agree that the role of the mentor is to:

   - Provide guidance, share ideas, and provide feedback.
   - Function as a sounding board for ideas/concerns about life choices.
   - Identify resources to help enhance personal development and career growth.
   - Serve as an advocate for the mentee whenever the opportunity presents itself.

5. We agree that the role of the mentee (you, the learner) is to:

   - Identify the skills, knowledge, and goals you want to achieve and communicate with your mentor.
   - Maintain a mentoring plan and work with your mentor to set goals, developmental activities, and time frames.
   - Work with your mentor to find resources for learning; identify people and information that might be helpful.

6. We agree to keep the content of these meetings confidential.
7. The mentor agrees to be honest and provide constructive feedback to the mentee. The mentee agrees to be open to feedback and say thank you. (The mentor can also mentor between one and four mentees.)

Date: _____

Mentor's signature: _____

Mentee's signature: _____

# GETTING TO KNOW YOU GUIDE

Name: _____

Position: _____

Time frame employed at the company: _____

Before we get started, let us get to know each other. By answering each of these questions, you will examine your skills, traits, competencies, and abilities before we start the mentoring program so I can best support you.

What is your first memory of wanting to teach?

_____

_____

_____

_____

_____

What interests you about leadership or administration?

_____

_____

_____

_____

_____

What is your favorite topic to learn or teach about?

_____

_____

_____

_____

_____

How would you describe your ideal workplace? Name at least three things that are important to you.

_____

_____

_____

_____

_____

What motivates you in your life?

_____

_____

_____

_____

_____

Where do you see yourself in five years?

_____

_____

_____

_____

_____

What life events have shaped you? What specifically from ages one to twelve?

_____

_____

_____

_____

_____

What technology did you grow up with and still use?

_____

_____

_____

_____

_____

How do you relate to people older than you? Younger than you?

_____

_____

_____

_____

_____

What concerns you?

_____

_____

_____

_____

_____

What do you want to accomplish after completing the mentorship program?

_____

_____

_____

_____

How can a mentor support you?

_____

_____

_____

_____

How do you want to be mentored?

_____

_____

_____

_____

_____

_____


What are your gifts?

_____ Customer service skills

_____ Soft skills (collaborator, discipline, humility, initiative, open to feedback, love to learn, positive attitude, etc.)

_____ Smart

_____ Creative

_____ Educational knowledge

_____ Organized

_____ Other_____


How do you learn best?

_____ Auditory (listening)

_____ Visual (seeing)

_____ Tactile-kinesthetic (hands-on)


What are three areas of development opportunities (weaknesses)?

a.

b.

c.


What is your preferred method of communication?

_____

_____

_____

_____

_____

What do you do for your health and well-being?

_____

_____

_____

_____

_____

What are some of your hobbies?

_____

_____

_____

_____

_____

What podcasts do you listen to or something you watch on TV?

_____

_____

_____

_____

_____

Let's create a weekly schedule.

Day of the week:

Time of the week:

Preferred method

- Face-to-face meeting
- Zoom technology
- Phone call

Thank you for completing the Getting to Know You Guide.

# SELF-ASSESSMENT

Let's begin by starting the self-assessment inventory and creating a structure to build upon. It is a step-by-step approach guided by a mentor.

If you are an employee reading this to improve your chances of getting promoted, please begin by completing the self-assessment. In the second column, rate yourself in each category from 1 to 10, 1 being poor and 10 being excellent. Do not skip any of the twenty-six categories. Save the third column for your weekly coaching meetings.

If you are the supervisor, schedule weekly mentoring meetings. Read through the questions before meeting with the employee to sense where you want to take the conversation. Feel free to answer the questions based on your school's culture and environment. This approach will help you mentor a new generation of aspiring leaders. Using this approach gives you a plan and process for which you can be responsible and a guide to your career.

**The A-to-Z Guide for Navigating the Journey to Educational Leadership**

Pre-Assessment Inventory

| ABCs for Growth and Development | On a scale of 1 to 10, with 1 being poor and 10 being excellent | Plan to improve/resources utilized |
| --- | --- | --- |
| Attitude | | |
| Brand | | |
| Communication | | |
| Decision-making | | |
| Energy | | |
| Focus | | |

| | | |
|---|---|---|
| Gratitude | | |
| Habits | | |
| Integrity | | |
| Jaded | | |
| Knowledge of the operation | | |
| Leadership | | |
| Mindset | | |
| Networking | | |
| Opportunity | | |
| Purpose | | |
| Questioning | | |
| Resiliency | | |
| Self-awareness | | |
| Thank you | | |
| Upskilling | | |
| Vision | | |
| White lies | | |
| Xper | | |
| Yearning | | |
| Zone | | |

# THE A-TO-Z PATHWAY FOR NAVIGATING THE JOURNEY TO EDUCATIONAL LEADERSHIP

## A is for Attitude

How essential do you think having a positive and professional attitude at work is? What is your attitude each day when you arrive at work? What about throughout the day? Do people like to be around you? Do you bring a positive outlook to the workspace, or do people avoid you? What is your attitude in traffic? What is your attitude when you are delayed? How do you manage it?

Do you bring down the team? Do people make excuses for you, such as saying, "Well, that is just how he or she is," and try to avoid you? Are you an energy drain on the team? Do not be a Debbie Downer or a Ned Know-It-All.

After authoring his book, *The Energy Bus*, Jon Gordon wrote an article called "How to Deal with Energy Vampires." The point is that you do not want to be known as an energy vampire—someone who sucks the air out of the room. You feel bored, overwhelmed, and frustrated by them. These people exist. Make sure you are not one of them. Remember, poor attitudes are contagious, and so are good ones. How would people you work with describe your attitude?

According to the dictionary, the definition of attitude is a way of thinking or feeling expressed through behaviors. You can express an attitude in various ways, such as job satisfaction, productivity, innovation, respect, helpfulness, and overall morale within the department.

Attitude is fundamental to your career success. We know it as a soft skill. There are many excellent assessments online that you could take to form a baseline if you do not feel you are as self-aware as you would like to be. Assessments can include attitude, emotional intelligence, leadership skills, etc. We all have blind spots, so the more you discover yours and take steps to improve, the more confident and promotable you become. Start each day with a gratitude journal or positive meditation or affirmations. The more consistent you are with starting each day like this, the more your attitude will improve. Taking small steps each day creates more significant attitude opportunities. Once you find the beauty in the little things, your universe seems to expand in higher proportion.

Surround yourself with positive people. Don't you love being around positive people? I know positive people inspire and motivate me. They make me smile. Do you make others smile?

Do excellent work, expecting nothing in return. Be willing to forgive. Learn from your mistakes, and do not beat yourself up mentally. When you make a mistake, get in the habit of thinking through what you learned and then move on. Do not dwell on negative things, people, or conversations. Part of my professional success is that I do not dwell on problems. I get into action and work toward a solution. My advice is to get into action, and a change in attitude will follow.

Charles R. Swindoll is well known for his quote on attitude. He says, "Life is 10 percent what happens to you and 90 percent how you react to it." So, we can change our attitudes. He said that the longer he lives, he realizes how imperative attitude is. It is more important than facts, past education, money, circumstances, appearance, skills, or what other people say and do. It will make or break a company, family, relationship, or church. We have a choice every day. What choices are you making, especially in times of stress? When driving in traffic? When things do not go well? When someone upsets you? What are you choosing?

John C. Maxwell authored *Attitude 101: What Every Leader Needs to Know.* This book is a practical guide and a wonderful place to examine your thoughts, feelings, and behaviors at work. You can determine your circumstances by maintaining a positive attitude. You can energize the team. You can take your first step toward leadership by improving your attitude at work, with family, and with friends. It starts with you.

*"A positive attitude gives you power over your circumstances instead of allowing your circumstances to have power over you."*

– Joyce Meyer

## Self-Assessment Questions

| Questions | Responses |
|---|---|
| How self-aware are you? | |
| Have you ever taken an attitude assessment? Have you ever had a 360-degree performance assessment in your career? If yes, what did it reveal? | |
| If you were to ask your peers about your attitude, what would they say? Interview five people you trust who will give you direct feed-back about your attitude. | |
| What would your supervisor say regarding your attitude? If you do not know, ask. | |
| What would your colleagues say about your attitude? | |
| If you have direct reports, what would they say? | |
| What would your family say about your attitude? | |
| When you hit a roadblock at work, how do you manage it? | |
| Do you feel like you are resilient? If yes, give an example. | |

| | |
|---|---|
| How do you get back on track if you get off track? | |
| Provide an example of when you chose a positive attitude in a stressful situation. | |
| In what area do you think you excel? | |
| What is one area in which you could improve your attitude? | |
| What is one action step you can take to improve in this area? | |
| How will you know you are making progress? | |

## Coach/Mentor Questions

| Questions | Responses |
|---|---|
| Describe your attitude self-assessment. | |
| Did you ask others for feedback about your attitude? | |
| Did you learn anything new? | |
| Did any comments surprise you? | |
| What is one action step you can take to improve your attitude? | |

| | |
|---|---|
| How will you measure your improvement in this area? | |
| How can I support you? | |

## B is for Brand

A brand is so much more than dressing for success. Your brand is all of your actions throughout the day. Imagine your brand as a collection of your accomplishments and goals, similar to a personal portfolio called *Me, Inc.* What does your brand say about you? What does your brand say to your organization each day? What impression do you think you are making? Are you consistent? Your brand includes how you dress, communicate, and carry yourself—your image. It is your content defined by your expertise and unique humanity, which is generosity, vulnerability, accountability, and candor (Ferrazzi & Raz, 2005). Your brand is your walking billboard of everything you do, communicate, project, and wear.

A brand is a way of marketing yourself in your career. So, you must be self-aware before you can build your brand in person and through social media. As you develop your career, you want to be known as a thought leader.

In social media, think about where you post and what you post. What would your employer say about these posts? Would they believe you show company values? Or would they think they had made an unwise decision hiring you? Your social media brand is your digital fingerprint and follows you throughout your career.

The reality is that your posts can help or harm your career. Some prospective employees were not offered positions because of Facebook and other social media postings. Examples of such posts are Saturday night bar shots, foul language, provocative dress, etc. Whether you like it or not, nothing is off the record. Big Brother really is watching.

On the other hand, other employers hired some prospective employees because of their strong brands, posts, and contributions on their social media accounts. Examples of posts include a professional photo of yourself, volunteer work such as the Food Bank, Habitat for Humanity, family outings, etc. These demonstrate strong values.

LinkedIn is the most effective business tool. Take the time to build your profile. Learn how to do this. There are books, online resources, other LinkedIn profiles, and LinkedIn University to help you. Do you have a professional photograph for your social media accounts? Is your resume updated? How strong are your connections? How did you invite them? How many groups do you belong to? What videos, articles, or pictures are you posting/sharing? Do you have a strong headline? Are you becoming known as a subject matter expert?

Do you blog or post so you can become a thought leader? Do you have solid recommendations for you on your LinkedIn profile? These recommendations on LinkedIn can enhance your career visibility opportunities. Choose wisely when asking for professional recommendations.

Many years ago, I worked for an organization as president of one of the operating units. The president of the parent corporation was leaving, and I knew him well. He knew my work well. I asked him for a LinkedIn recommendation when I was setting up my profile. Honestly, I never thought about it again. Fast-forward six years, I had left my company and was interviewing for a new position with a new company. The company flew me to Chicago for a face-to-face interview. While waiting, the Human Resources recruiter met and talked with me. The first thing she said was, "I checked out your LinkedIn profile. You have impressive recommendations." I had forgotten about those recommendations. The man who was going to interview me for a new position with a new company was the former president of the parent corporation I had worked for those many years ago. This recommendation helped me get an opportunity to interview. Oh, and yes, I got the new job.

Beyond social media is your brand at work. How do you show up? Are you helpful? Do you consistently do your best work? Do you dress professionally every day? Do you read your emails before hitting send to ensure there are no typos? Do you send professional messages? No one can be an expert in everything, so ask questions. Seek more experienced people and learn from them. Seek thought leaders and see what they are doing. You are unique, so capitalize on your strengths.

There are so many great places to learn how to improve your brand. In 2004, Fast Company magazine featured the article "The Brand Called You" by Tom Peters. To deepen your understanding, check out this article to learn how to improve your brand. Your brand is your reputation every day. https://www.fastcompany.com/28905/brand-called-you

*"Your brand is what people say about you when you are not in the room."*

– Jeff Bezos, Amazon

## Self-Assessment Questions

| Questions | Responses |
|---|---|
| What does your brand communicate about you? | |
| What would people say about you if you were not in the room? If you do not know, ask trusted friends and colleagues and find out. | |
| How self-aware are you? 1 being poor and 10 being excellent. | |
| On a scale of 1–10, with 1 being poor and 10 being excellent, how strong is your brand? Face-to-face Communication Social media accounts | |
| What is one area in which you could improve your brand at work? | |
| Have you set up a LinkedIn profile? How can it be improved? | |
| What is one area in which you could improve your brand on your social media accounts? Is there anything you have posted in the past that might have you concerned? | |
| How will you learn more about developing your personal brand? | |
| What is one action step you can take to improve your brand? | |
| How will you know you are making progress? | |

## Coach/Mentor Questions

| Questions | Responses |
|---|---|
| Describe your brand's self-assessment. | |
| What did you learn from the *Fast Company* article "The Brand Called You" by Tom Peters? | |
| Did you ask others for feedback at work? What did you learn? | |
| Did you ask others for feedback on your social media accounts? | |
| Did you learn anything new? | |
| Did any comments surprise you? | |
| After a review of your LinkedIn profile, I think I can offer some suggestions. Are you open to this type of feedback? | |
| What is one action you can take to improve in this area? | |
| How will you measure your improvement in this area? | |
| How can I support you? | |

## C is for Communication

Communication means listening to understand others fully and effectively by presenting information and ideas using oral, written, visual, and nonverbal communication skills. How effective are your communication skills? People judge others within seconds, often based on speaking skills. Do you relate well to peers, staff members, managers, and senior management? Do you struggle with how to get your meaning across to others? Do you get nervous? Do you overshare details about your personal life at work?

Depending on your communication level, check out the following organizations to enhance your confidence and communication skills: Dale Carnegie Training, Toastmasters International, and National Speakers Association (NSA) in your area. Dale Carnegie is an excellent organization specializing in public-speaking training and is found in most major cities. Toastmasters International is an influential organization to join in your local area to practice your speaking skills. The National Speakers Association is for professional speakers and those who often speak in leadership positions.

What about your writing skills? Are your emails, texts, and presentations clear and appropriate for the intended receiver or audience? Have you ever created confusion with your poorly worded emails and texts? Do you read and use spell-check and resources such as Grammarly© before hitting the send button? If writing is a weakness, it can improve with deliberate practice. We can all improve our communication skills regardless of our organizational role. There are many significant online resources to help you improve, so check them out. You do not want to create a negative impression from behind your computer without ever leaving your office.

What about your listening skills? Do you wait for the person to finish what they are saying before you talk or interrupt? Do you give unsolicited advice? Do you try to multitask? Are you thinking about what you will say without paying attention to what the other person is saying? Have you learned to ask questions instead of always talking? This skill takes practice.

Here are some tips for better listening:

- Listen, do not talk.
- Avoid interruptions.
- 10 percent talking.
- Related conversation.
- Do not offer advice.
- Be aware of your environment.
- Take appropriate notes if required.

Which one of these seven tips is a struggle for you?

Communication can go astray very fast at work. If you do not think so, have you ever played the telephone game? It is a game for five or more people. You whisper something to the first person, and they must repeat it in a whisper to the next person. By the time you reach the fifth person, the original statement is not the same. The slow and subtle changes in information are how rumors start in organizations because of poor listening skills and rephrasing. As your listening improves, so will all your relationships. Personal development classes offer to help you improve in this area.

While all these skills are critical to career success, most communication models suggest that 7 percent is verbal and 93 percent of our communication is nonverbal. The 93 percent breaks down into 55 percent body language and 38 percent tone of voice (Yaffe, 2011). There are obvious communication barriers, including language, culture, and differences in time and place. Where do you struggle?

Poor communication skills create problems at work for you and the organization. How would you assess yourself after reviewing **A**-Attitude, **B**-Brand, and **C**-Communication? Where are your opportunities for self-improvement? You have taken the first three steps to become more aware of who you are and can become. Let us keep going!

*"The art of communication is the language of leadership."*

– James Humes

## Self-Assessment Questions

| Questions | Responses |
|---|---|
| Rate your communication skills on a scale of 1–10, with 1 being poor and 10 being excellent.<br>_____Listening<br>_____Speaking<br>_____Writing<br>_____Presenting<br>_____Facilitating<br>_____Nonverbal communication<br>_____Body language<br>_____Tone of voice | |
| What is one area you need to start working on first? | |
| What is one area you could improve your communication skills at work? | |
| What outside resources will help you improve in this area? | |
| Have you ever participated in Toastmasters, Dale Carnegie, National Speakers Association, or personal-development courses to improve communication? | |
| How will you know you are making progress? | |

**Coach/Mentor Questions**

| Questions | Responses |
|---|---|
| Describe your communication skill strengths. | |
| Describe your communication skill developmental opportunities. | |
| How important do you think effective communication skills are for our organization? | |
| Have you ever participated in Toastmasters, Dale Carnegie, National Speakers Association, or personal-development courses to improve your communication? | |
| Are you open to joining a local Toastmasters group? | |
| What is one action you can take to improve in this area? | |
| How will you measure your improvement in this area? | |
| How can I support you? | |

## D is Decision-Making

What decision-making process do you use? Would you love to share a model that works for you? It might be a mode you are familiar with or something new to you. If you are working at an institution that has a business department, you might be familiar with the Lean process certification, Kaizen, or Six Sigma Green Belt programs. One model taught is the PDCA: Plan, Do, Check, Act. Think about something you need to decide where you can apply the method.

David Stokes (2019) explains the process in more detail:

- *Plan* is where you set the objectives and processes to deliver the desired results.
- *Do* is the phase where you would enact the plan created and test minor changes to gather data to determine the effectiveness of the changes.
- *Check* the results of your plan and evaluate any minor changes against your expected outcomes or obvious comparison.
- *Act* is where you can improve the process, such as addressing problems or opportunities for improvement.

You might have relied on your experience and good track record of deciding, which has served you well to date. You decide daily for your class, teaching, pacing class activities, student behaviors, learning outcomes, etc. Once you take on an administrator role, things operate at a different level. So, in what areas can you use this model? A new project, designing a new process or service, degree program, curriculum review, advisory committee, retention plan, any change initiative, or continuous improvement?

It is helpful to be open to new possibilities and have a growth mindset, which means letting go of assumptions and what you know. In education, it is critical not to wait; problems only worsen, so be proactive. Just because things have been working, do not accept the status quo. Take classes, network, learn from others, and research best practices.

Know that your original plan will probably be iterative and must adapt over time. Look for solutions. As an administrator, bring in others to contribute and create a work environment where people feel valued, respected, and appreciated. Conduct a root cause analysis during a group discussion and ask "why" five times. Have fun and use creativity in these meetings. Make a commitment to continuous improvement. Conduct periodic debriefs on what went well and what needs to be improved. Document as you go, year after year, and you and your team will grow!

*"In any moment of decision, the best thing you can do is the right thing, the next best thing is the wrong thing, and the worst thing is to do nothing."*

–Theodore Roosevelt

## Self-Assessment Questions

| Questions | Responses |
|---|---|
| What decision-making process do you use? Explain. | |
| What is one area you can use the PDCA model? | |
| What is step one for your plan you want to address? | |
| What is step two, which is do? | |
| What is step three—check for your plan? | |
| What is step four for the issue you are addressing? | |
| How is this approach different from what you have used in the past? | |
| Where can you use this model in the future? | |
| How will you measure your improvement in this area? | |
| How can I support you in using this model? | |

**Coach/Mentor Questions**

| Questions | Responses |
|---|---|
| What decision-making process do you use? Explain. | |
| What is one area you can use the PDCA model? | |
| What is step one for your plan you want to address? | |
| What is step two for the area you want to focus on, which is do? | |
| What is step three—check for your plan? | |
| What is step four for the issue you are addressing? | |
| How is this approach different from what you have used in the past? | |
| Where can you use this model in the future? | |
| How will you measure your improvement in this area? | |
| How can I support you in using this model? | |

# E is for Energy

Do you possess energy that draws people to you, or do you bring down the group because of your lack of energy? Think about people in your life to whom you are attracted because of their energy. How did you come across them?

How can you change this if your energy level is low? Are you taking care of yourself? Do you meditate? Do you exercise? Do you eat healthily? Do you drink enough water? Do you get enough sleep? Do you think these healthy habits are important?

Start taking better care of yourself. Working in education takes a great deal of energy; in this business, people skip taking care of themselves because they are taking care of others. Plan out meals so you can better maintain a healthy lifestyle. Drink water throughout the day. Stop drinking sugary drinks or souped-up energy drinks; they do not help energy levels. If you start to feel your energy subsiding, breathe.

Do you surround yourself with positive and forward-thinking people? Do you take vacations to rejuvenate? Do you carve out downtime to recapture your creativity? Do you keep yourself inspired by quotes, books, and affirmations? Do you have a hobby you are enthusiastic about that fulfills you? Do you approach life as the glass is half empty rather than half full and think this is all there is to life? Do you feel resilient at work? Do you feel loved in your relationships? Do you have a spiritual practice that uplifts you? What are you passionate about in life, or what do you want? Do you know your life's purpose? What are the possibilities in your life? What goals and actions have you put in place?

Once you tap into answering these questions, your energy level will begin to improve. Think about a time when your energy was high. You could do anything and tackle anything, like being in the zone. What caused the elevated level of energy? What were you doing at the time that made you feel energized? Consider the possibility that you were acting on things important to you.

Finally, get enough sleep to tackle the next day with the energy level that serves you best. Too many people at work are sleep-deprived, which is a real problem. According to Larry Alton (2016), a professional blogger and researcher, there is a relationship between sleep and worker productivity. We all need and want more sleep but cannot always obtain a quality night's sleep. Pay attention to what works for you. Give yourself permission to go to bed earlier to enjoy eight hours of sleep. Stop eating three hours before bed. Ensure you turn off all electronic devices at least an hour before bed to reduce stimulation. Make certain you have a good mattress, a dark room, and the right room temperature. These should assist in giving you the energy to tackle the day ahead.

If you are a person who wakes up in the middle of the night consumed by thoughts, have a journal and pen by your bed. Write the thoughts down and go back to sleep. You can train your brain to know there is a system for capturing thoughts; this can settle your mind so you can go back to sleep. Journaling is more effective than lying in bed, thinking, not being able to sleep, and then getting up in the morning more tired than when you went to bed the night before.

Remember, you are worth it!

*"And what is a man without energy? Nothing—nothing at all."*

– Mark Twain

## Self-Assessment Questions

| Questions | Responses |
|---|---|
| How would you rate your energy level on a scale of 1–10, with 1 being poor and 10 being excellent? | |
| What personal energy areas could be improved upon?<br><br>_____Healthy eating<br>_____Exercise daily<br>_____Drinking more water<br>_____Sleeping at least 8 hours a night<br>_____Relationships<br>_____Setting goals | |
| What is an area of interest to start on first? | |
| What actions will you take? | |
| How will you know you are making progress? | |

## Coach/Mentor Questions

| Questions | Responses |
|---|---|
| Describe your personal energy level at this point in your life. | |
| How can you improve your energy level based on your personal assessment? | |
| In what area will you start?<br>_____Healthy eating<br>_____Exercise daily<br>_____Drinking more water<br>_____Sleeping at least 8 hours a night<br>_____Relationships<br>_____Setting goals | |
| Do you feel you surround yourself with positive people who add to your life? If anyone might be toxic to you, what will you do about it? | |
| What are you passionate about? What goals have you set for yourself? | |
| What do you want your life to stand for? | |
| What do you want in your life? | |
| How will you measure your improvement in this area? | |
| How can I support you? | |

## F is for Focus

While it is sometimes difficult to focus in this fast-paced world with competing priorities, deadlines, social media, etc., it is imperative. Our attention spans are becoming shorter and shorter, but it is possible to work on improving your focus. While we all have been told that multitasking is excellent, you can only do one thing at a time well.

When you get to the office, get ready to work. Focus on the most urgent items, then the essential projects for the day. Stop avoiding or procrastinating on critical tasks or problems; it only adds stress to your life. Save the less important tasks for later in the day when your energy level might be less. You will find you are more productive and more fulfilled each day.

Make a list of things that distract you and keep them to a minimum or eliminate them. Block out time on your calendar for projects. Schedule the deadline date on the calendar and work backward to make sure you fulfill your part of the project on time. Do not schedule every minute of the day. Take brief breaks every so often to reenergize.

Do not log into your social media accounts while at work unless that is your job. They distract and eat up valuable time. If your job allows, block out time to check email only three times a day. Answer the emails, delete them, or file them for follow-up. Deal with emails one at a time. Also, I have noticed that some people waste a lot of time talking to coworkers for long periods, thus wasting valuable work time. While it may seem like a good idea, you pay for it by working later to get your work done to catch up. Wasting time creates more stress and anxiety because you run out of time. If procrastinating or wasting time has become a habit, analyze the reason. Do you enjoy the adrenaline rush? Some people seem to live this way without stopping to see if they can change how they manage their lives.

So, when you begin the day, have a plan. Take stock of what you want to accomplish. List the time-wasters. Reflect on where you need to bring more focus in your professional life and personal life. Breathe and get started.

*You can do anything as long as you have the passion, the drive, the focus, and the support.*

– Sabrina Bryan

## Self-Assessment Questions

| Questions | Responses |
|---|---|
| Is being focused a strength or a challenge for you? | |
| In what areas are you distracted? | |
| Do you think you are an adrenaline junkie? | |
| How can you mitigate these distractions from happening? | |
| What is your plan to address this? | |
| How do you start your day and focus on the top priority items? | |
| Do you use a digital calendar system for everything you are accountable for? | |
| What is one action step you can put in place today? | |
| How will you know you are making progress? | |

**Coach/Mentor Questions**

| Questions | Responses |
|---|---|
| How do you stay focused for the day? | |
| What are areas of distraction for you? | |
| How can you mitigate these? | |
| What is your plan to address this? | |
| How do you start your day and focus on the top priority items? | |
| Do you use a digital calendar system for everything you are accountable for? | |
| How will you measure your improvement in this area? | |
| How can I support you? | |

## G is for Gratitude

Gratitude is being thankful. How many times each day do we miss the opportunity to be grateful? Did you know that by practicing gratitude, your life has more meaning? It changes your perspective.

Set aside time each day and start by being grateful for at least three things in your life. Either say them aloud or write them down. Keeping a gratitude journal by your bed is extremely helpful to start and continue this practice. Putting pen to paper is a powerful tool that activates your brain and senses.

So often, we cannot acknowledge the small things we are blessed to have or that happen in our lives. Many people focus on what is wrong. If you take the opposite approach and look for things for which to be grateful, you will find more and more blessings. Bring in all your senses as you write or state what you are grateful for. How does it make you feel? What do you see? What do you hear? What about a sense of touch?

So, what does expressing gratitude have to do with promotability? Everything. When you are in business, there are a series of problems to solve, which cause stress. According to Robert Emmons (2004), a world's leading gratitude expert and psychology professor at the University of California Davis, "Gratitude can be that stress buster." It allows you to generate optimism while building strength to recover quicker from setbacks. Let people in your life know you are grateful for them. Appreciate your coworkers for their contributions.

Lindsey Holmes (2017), the deputy editor for the *Huffington Post*, says more gratitude equals a better life. That means a better life at home and work. If you build this habit over thirty days, you will feel grateful. Your whole outlook on life will be improved. Pass it on!

For further inspiration, read the gratitude poem "I Am Thankful For" by Nancy J. Carmody and share it with your team. It will reset your perspective. In addition, watch the YouTube video by Warhawk Matt Scott, "No Excuses" https://www.youtube.com/watch?v=obdd31Q9PqA

*"Gratitude makes sense of our past, brings peace for today, and creates a vision for tomorrow."*

– Melody Beattie

## Self-Assessment Questions

| Questions | Responses |
|---|---|
| What did you think about gratitude research in your life and its effect? | |
| Do you have a daily routine of expressing and showing gratitude? Provide a few examples. | |
| Do you keep a gratitude journal? | |
| Would you be willing to write what you are grateful for each morning? | |
| What did you think of the gratitude poem and the YouTube video? How did they change your perspective? | |
| In what areas of your life have you taken people or situations for granted? | |
| What is one action step you can put into place today regarding gratitude? | |
| How will you know you are making progress? | |

## Coach/Mentor Questions

| Questions | Responses |
|---|---|
| What did you think about gratitude research in your life and its effect? | |
| Do you have a daily routine of expressing and showing gratitude? Provide a few examples. | |
| What did you think of the gratitude poem and the YouTube video? How did it change your perspective? | |
| What are you grateful for at work? | |
| What are you grateful for at home? | |
| What are you grateful for from your work team? | |
| What are you grateful for in your relationships? | |
| What daily practice are you willing to take to keep gratitude at the forefront? | |
| Is there any area of your life or a person you have taken for granted? | |
| How will you measure your improvement in this area? | |
| How can I support you? | |

**I Am Thankful For** by Nancy J Carmody (2002)

I am thankful for
.....the mess to clean up after a party
because it means I have been surrounded by friends.
.....the taxes that I pay
because it means that I'm employed.
.....the clothes that fit a little too snug
because it means I have enough to eat.
.....my shadow who watches me work
because it means I am out in the sunshine.
.....the spot I find at the far end of the parking lot
because it means I am capable of walking.
.....all the complaining I hear about our government
because it means we have freedom of speech.
.....that lady behind me in church who sings off key
because it means that I can hear.
.....lawn that needs mowing, windows that need cleaning, and gutters that need fixing
because it means I have a home.
.....my huge heating bill
because it means that I am warm.
.....weariness and aching muscles at the end of the day
because it means that I have been productive.
.....the alarm that goes off in the early morning hours
because it means that I am alive.

## H is for Habits

Do you possess good habits or bad habits? What would your friends, family, or coworkers say about your habits? Interview a few trusted friends and colleagues to get an honest assessment. Often, we are blind to what we do and how it affects others.

Once again, Fast Company published a research article in 2017 on bad habits to ditch. "Ditch These Seven Bad Habits Before 2018 Starts" by Gwen Moran can be found at https://www.fastcompany.com/40503547/ditch-these-seven-bad-habits-before-2018-starts. Do you possess any of these habits?

Once we learn to recognize our bad habits, how can we start to change them? We all have them. You cannot change everything overnight, but you can take steps to improve one thing at a time. Describe your bad habit. What do you think is the root cause of it? If you were to change it, how would it benefit your life? With what will you replace the bad habit? What can you do instead?

Once you have identified the habit, the root cause, and with what you can replace the bad habit, next is accountability. Reach out to a coworker or friend and have them be your accountability partner. Give yourself some time. Much has been written on this subject about how long it takes to change a habit. The time frame ranges from 21 days to three months. It depends on the habit and the person. Commit to the time frame. Know that you probably will make a few mistakes along the way or backslide; we are human, but do not quit. No need to justify the reasons it happened but realize what triggered it. Recommit yourself to make progress toward changing the habit. Another great resource is *Atomic Habits* by James Clear and *Chop Wood and Carry Water* by Joshua Metcalf. Remember, tomorrow is a new day!

Realize that many habits you possess are positive. Keep them and discard what does not serve you and others. You are on the road to excellence.

*"We are what we repeatedly do. Excellence then is not an act but a habit."*

– Aristotle

## Self-Assessment Questions

| Questions | Responses |
|---|---|
| What habits need to change? | |
| What is the habit you are going to work on first? | |
| What is the underlying cause of poor habits? | |
| Are you willing to have an accountability partner? If so, who could be your partner? | |
| What is your time frame for committing to change the habit? | |
| How will you know you are making progress? | |
| How will you celebrate your success? | |

## Coach/Mentor Questions

| Questions | Responses |
|---|---|
| What habit have you decided to work on first? | |
| How will it lead to excellence? | |
| What is the benefit of making this change? | |
| What will it cost you if you do not make the change? | |
| How will you feel when you change this habit? | |
| Do you have an accountability partner? | |
| How will you keep this present at the top of your mind daily? | |
| What is your time frame? | |
| If you make a misstep, how will you recover and get back on track? | |
| How will you measure your improvement in this area? | |
| How will we celebrate your success? | |
| How can I support you? | |

## I is for Integrity

Integrity is always doing what you say, regardless of whether anyone is watching you or knows. It is the state of being in the integrity of self—keeping and honoring your word, your promises to yourself, your friends, family, and coworkers. It will amaze you how free you feel when you know you can keep your word to yourself and others, and they can count on you. It does not mean always saying yes.

Here is a situation to consider. Are you great at work at keeping your word, but when it comes to yourself, not so much—or vice versa? Take an honest look at your life and decide where you can improve your integrity muscle. It will take practice, but you grow each day you try. Now, to make this trait real, you need to dig deep and tell the truth to yourself.

Here are some areas to think about:

- Do you gossip about others?
- Have you taken things without paying for them?
- Have you taken office supplies home for personal use?
- Have you used the company copier to copy personal things?
- Do you tell little white lies and justify them?
- Do you exceed the speed limit?
- Do you text and drive?
- Have you ever parked in a handicapped accessible parking space, even though you are not handicapped?
- Do you think the rules do not apply to you?
- Have you hurt someone's feelings and never apologized?
- Have you been charged less for an item at a store and failed to tell them they charged you the wrong amount?
- Have you ever found money on the floor at a store and failed to turn it in?
- Have you disclosed confidential information about your company or a project?
- Have you used work time on social media when you were supposed to be working?
- Have you ever made a mistake at work and failed to own it?
- Did you fail to meet a company deadline?
- Do you follow company policies 100 percent of the time?
- Have you taken credit for someone else's work?
- Have you ever compromised your values?
- Do you have the courage to tell the truth?
- Are you great at keeping your word with others but not as much with yourself?
- Do you have integrity in yourself?

- Do you keep your word to yourself? For example, do you tell yourself you will go to the gym three days a week and then not follow through?
- Do you tell yourself that you want to seek an opportunity to be promoted but do not share this goal with your manager or take the steps to be ready to apply?

Look to see where there are opportunities to improve each day in this area. So how can you build your integrity muscle?

Be honest. When you make a mistake, own it. Be a person of your word. Become someone everyone can count on, no matter what. Know that you can rely on yourself. Know that you are your word. The more you practice the integrity muscle, the stronger you become. It is just like working out. You know you have arrived when you can count on your word and yourself. Integrity is a crucial characteristic of leadership.

Good luck getting stronger each day!

*"A single lie destroys a whole reputation of integrity."*

– Baltasar Gracian

## Self-Assessment Questions

| Questions | Responses |
|---|---|
| What does integrity mean to you? | |
| Is integrity important in a leadership role? | |
| When you read the examples, did you see yourself in any of them? | |
| Whom do you admire because of their integrity? What company displays integrity? | |
| What examples are you aware of when the leader failed to have integrity in business? What happened? If none come to mind, research and share. | |
| What is one area that you can work on for yourself? | |
| How do you justify your behavior when your integrity is not intact? | |
| How will you know you are making progress? | |
| How will you know when you can keep your word? To yourself? To others? | |

## Coach/Mentor Questions

| Questions | Responses |
|---|---|
| What does integrity mean to you? | |
| What did you think of some examples provided? Let us discuss a few things. | |
| Have you ever looked at integrity in this way? What surprised you? | |
| If you were in a leadership position, how would you model it? | |
| In your current position, how do you demonstrate integrity? | |
| What happens when a leader does not model integrity? What happened to the organization? To the culture? To the people? Can you give me some specific examples? | |
| How will you measure your improvement in this area? | |
| How can I support you? | |

## J is for Jaded

Are you jaded because of all the world events? Are you feeling cynical about leadership? Do you feel disappointed by athletes and people in the media? Do you think life is unfair, and they have passed you over? Do you complain about *those* people at work? Are you the person sitting in the stands and yelling but doing nothing, or do you see a situation and want to become an agent of change? Do you complain about your job, coworkers, or boss? Or do you take the high road? Do you get involved in your community to improve the quality of life? Do you engage others to join you? Who are you in these scenarios? Are you in the stands or on the field?

According to the Merriam-Webster Dictionary, jaded is feeling "dull or cynical." Do you feel entitled to be cynical because they have wronged you at work? Do you feel like people at work are not doing their part? Did you know that being cynical is a defensive posture to try and protect yourself? However, being cynical can dramatically decrease the quality and health of your life. When you see the world from this perspective, everything is dull, and there is no joy. The only person suffering is you. So, if there is an opportunity for a promotion at your workplace, what reason would leadership have for promoting someone cynical? I cannot think of any, can you?

If you want to take the path to have the possibility of being promoted, you can take a different approach and improve the quality of your life. You can take the high road, become a change agent, and become more positive. You can become compassionate toward others. Instead of looking for what is wrong in every situation, begin looking for what is right. Decide who you want to be. Your future is in your hands!

*"I suppose there are many reasons to be jaded or sarcastic, but I hang on to the reasons why life is beautiful."*

– Kellie O'Hara

## Self-Assessment Questions

| Questions | Responses |
|---|---|
| On a scale of 1 to 10, with 1 being *jaded* all the time and 10 being *never feeling jaded,* how would you rate yourself?<br><br>_____Jaded | |
| In what areas do you struggle with cynicism (believe people are generally selfish and dishonest)? | |
| How can you change this outlook? | |
| How will you know you are shifting your perspective? | |

## Coach/Mentor Questions

| Questions | Responses |
|---|---|
| Are there areas at work where you feel jaded? What happened? | |
| What is the root cause? | |
| How can you change your perspective? | |
| If you have a direct report who is jaded, how would you coach that employee? How can you propose an alternative perspective? | |
| What strategies might work to improve the situation? | |
| What resources might be available? | |
| How can I support your growth in this area? | |

## K is for Knowledge

What are some traits and skills necessary for success in higher education?
Are you:

- Friendly, outgoing, people-oriented?
- Energetic and creative?
- A people person?
- Do you have a service leader attitude?
- Do you like to learn new things?

Have you ever considered becoming a program chair, committee chair, faculty development director, or a dean? What would it take to get there?

How well do you know all aspects of your role in the company? How well do you know the entire organization's operations? What do you need to know? What skills do you need that you may lack? Are there certifications or education that would enhance your promotability? Decide what you want to learn. Do you want to go wide or deep? Do you want to specialize in an area? Develop a plan to gain the knowledge you need to fill the gaps.

We defined knowledge as facts, information, and skills you learn through education and experience. How can you increase your knowledge? You can read. You can ask questions. You can seek a mentor or business coach. Is there training available to enhance your skill set, either inside the company or outside? Is there a professional organization you could join?

What can you volunteer to learn? You can stretch yourself and take on new projects to learn and assist others. Keep an open mind. It takes time to learn new things. You will make mistakes but learn from them. Notice how you feel when you are learning new things. It may be uncomfortable for a while as you are outside your comfort zone.

How can you continue to enhance your technology skills? Technology may be an area where you excel, but there is always more to learn, and it changes daily. You can also help others in this area if it is not their area of expertise. When the student becomes the teacher, you begin the path of mastery.

Examine other areas in your organization where you may need to learn:

- What is the company culture?
- What are the mission, vision, and values?
- Is the company strategic plan and goals available to you?
- Do you understand the financial aspects of the company you work for?
- Have you mastered finance in your life?
- Have you read the annual report of the company if publicly traded? Do you understand it?
- Do you know the accreditation standards?

- Do you know what reports are important in your company? Can you interpret what they mean?
- Do you know how the metrics can be achieved?
- Do you take part in deliberate practice and set aside time to master a new skill?
- What information is missing for you to increase your mastery?
- What is the company promotion protocol?

The only way to learn is to read, talk, practice, and then show mastery over time.

**Self-Assessment Questions**

| Questions | Responses |
| --- | --- |
| Where do you see your career in education? What are your long-term career goals? | |
| What certification, training, or education do you need to progress in your career? | |
| What did you learn from this section that you did not know? | |
| How knowledgeable are you about the education industry? | |
| What area do you need to learn more about in the industry? | |
| What is one action step you can take to improve in this area? | |
| How will you know you are making progress? | |

## Coach/Mentor Questions

| Questions | Responses |
|---|---|
| Where do you see your career in education? What are your long-term career goals? | |
| What certification, training, or education do you need to progress in your career? | |
| What did you learn from this section that you did not know? | |
| How knowledgeable are you about the education industry? | |
| What area do you need to learn more about in the industry? | |
| What is one action step you can take to improve in this area? | |
| How will you know you are making progress? | |
| How can you all support each other? | |
| How can I support you? | |

## L is for Leadership

How do you define leadership? According to McKinsey & Company (2022), leadership is a set of behaviors used to help people align their collective direction, to execute strategic plans, and continually renew an organization. Think about outstanding leaders in your present and the past. Who are they? What qualities and behaviors do they have? What qualities and behaviors do you want to emulate?

Congratulations on considering leadership education as the right path for you. Believe it or not, it is a skill to be learned. You do not have to be born with it. While there are many leadership styles that you can read about, leadership is more about behaviors. Nelson Mandela certainly was a born leader. He had a passion for making a difference. He had specific thinking patterns and perspectives. He had poise under pressure and in complex situations. Mandela also had projection when he entered a room. None of us are Mandela, and we should be true to ourselves. You can consider certain behaviors such as a passion for making a difference, respect and high regard for people, being supportive, possessing excellent communication skills, having well-developed emotional intelligence, operating with a strong results orientation, understanding and seeking different perceptions, and being an effective problem solver.

Unfortunately, some of the best lessons I have learned have been from poor leaders. In every situation, I told myself what I could learn from this leader about what not to do and tucked that information away for the day I would be a leader. It has served me well.

Leaders are readers. Great resources to increase your understanding of leadership include:

- *Become a Leader: Develop Executive Presence* by Charles Herman
- *Emotional Intelligence 2.0* by Travis Bradberry
- *Dare to Lead* by Brene Brown
- *Leadership IQ* by Mark Murphy
- *52 Weeks of Exceptional Leadership* by Kim Nugent
- *The Power of Positive Leadership* by Jon Gordon
- John Maxwell's books and training classes on leadership
- Current-day podcasts and TED Talks on the subject

Leadership is a journey and not a destination. You will make mistakes along the way and learn as you go.

*"It is better to lead from behind and to put others in front, especially when you celebrate victory when nice things occur. You take the front line when there is danger. Then people will appreciate your leadership."*

– Nelson Mandela

## Self-Assessment Questions

| Questions | Responses |
|---|---|
| What leaders do you admire? | |
| What poor lessons in leadership have you learned? | |
| What leadership skills or behaviors describe you? | |
| Where is at least one area that needs development? | |
| What was the last personal-development course you took? | |
| What podcasts or TED Talks have you listened to in the last year? | |
| What was the last book you read or listened to? | |
| What is the next leadership learning activity you will take on? | |

## Coach/Mentor Questions

| Questions | Responses |
| --- | --- |
| What leaders do you admire? | |
| What poor lessons in leadership have you learned? | |
| What leadership skills or behaviors describe you? | |
| Where is at least one area that needs development? | |
| What was the last personal-development course you took? | |
| What podcasts or TED Talks have you listened to in the last year? | |
| What was the last book you read or listened to? | |
| What is the next leadership learning activity you will take on? | |
| What do you want for yourself? | |
| Are you ready for the next opportunity? | |
| What are you going to do next? | |
| How can I support you on this journey? | |

## M is for Mindset

Do you have a fixed mindset or a growth mindset? How do you know? When you make a mistake, do you think you should stop or quit because you failed? Do you avoid risk and challenges? What do you tell yourself? When you are learning something new, and it is challenging and does not come quickly, what is your self-talk? Do you say, "It is something new to learn"? Do you want to be praised for the effort or the journey?

We define mindset as a set of attitudes one possesses. One of the best resources about mindset is Carol Dweck's book *Mindset: The New Psychology of Success: How We Can Fulfill our Potential.* Read it or Google it and see how you can develop a growth mindset in all areas of your life. Dr. Carol Dweck describes a fixed mindset as static, avoids challenges, sees the effort as fruitless, ignores useful negative feedback, and feels threatened by the success of others. She then describes the characteristics of a growth mindset. They are the desire to learn, embrace challenges, be persistent, learn from criticism, and be inspired by others. Who are you?

Let us test your mindset with a riddle.

> *Bobby and his father are in a horrible car accident, which instantly kills his father. Bobby is seriously injured and rushed to the hospital. The surgeon takes one look at Bobby on the operating table and says, "Oh my God! I can't operate on this boy. He is my son!"*

How can this be? What is the point of this riddle? The answer thirty years ago was that the surgeon was his mother. Today, the answer could also be his other father.

I tested Carol Dweck's mindset theory when facilitating a new graduate-student orientation workshop each session. We had a lot of interactive activities, so the students could get a feel for what they were about to undertake in obtaining a master's degree. About midway through the orientation, I gave the graduate students an assignment. I told them that at our university, we expect every student to use American Psychological Association (APA) formatting in referencing all sources for their papers. I handed out a research paper to each student and had them try to find the APA errors. This assignment was tough because they had not even started their classes. I watched with intrigue at how they approached the task. Most took the paper and tried to figure something out. A few took the paper and threw it to the side in total frustration. I did not let the exercise go over two minutes for fear of them leaving before they started.

I then conducted a debrief. I asked the students how they felt when I handed out the assignment. Some said they were scared, some were open to trying, and some felt like quitting. I told them to realize they were in graduate school to learn new things. I told them I did not expect them to do the assignment. I asked them to remember their feelings when we did this throughout their graduate school journey.

I wanted to create a growth mindset for every person in the workshop. They would not need graduate school if they already knew how to do these things. It is a place to learn, be challenged, and make mistakes. I then handed out an APA guide to help them do the assignment. We then reviewed the paper, and I noted the APA errors.

As I explained the difference and my intention, the students relaxed. They said it was a lesson they would never forget.

Let us take this to the business setting and your career. What is your mindset? I often heard colleagues say:

"This place is political."

"My boss is pressuring me to do____."

"I cannot get ahead here because I am____."

I know I have never said those things, as I do not see the world that way. It is not my mindset or my self-talk. I am sure there are workplaces where this exists, but is it really that way, or is it a fixed mindset to justify your situation and make them wrong? Truly, you are the only person who knows. As you read this, you may take issue with me, but a coach challenges your thinking.

*"Innovation requires an experimental mindset."*

– Denise Morrison

## Self-Assessment Questions

| Questions | Responses |
|---|---|
| Overall, do you feel you have a growth or a fixed mindset? | |
| In what areas of your life do you have a growth mindset? | |
| In what areas of your life do you have a fixed mindset? | |
| Do you like to be rewarded for the outcome or the journey? | |
| What do you say to yourself when things are hard or when you are learning something for the first time? | |
| How can you shift your mindset to a growth mindset? | |
| How will you know you are starting to shift your perspective? | |

## Coach/Mentor Questions

| Questions | Responses |
|---|---|
| Describe what you think is a growth mindset. | |
| Describe what you think is a fixed mindset. | |

| | |
|---|---|
| Do you feel you have a growth mindset or a fixed mindset? | |
| In what areas of your life do you have a growth mindset? | |
| In what areas of your life do you have a fixed mindset? | |
| Do you like to be rewarded for the outcome or the journey? Explain. | |
| What do you say to yourself when things are hard or when you are learning something for the first time? | |
| How can you shift your mindset to a growth mindset? | |
| How will you know you are shifting your perspective? | |
| How can I encourage your growth in this area? | |
| We are halfway through the twenty-six traits. What do you feel you have learned to date? | |
| How do you feel you have changed? | |

## N is for Networking

What is networking? Networking is where you develop business relationships, share information, and assist each other. What is important for building a network? Building a strong professional network is part of your career strategy. People in your network can give you advice. Determine what your target audience is. Not all events are going to be right for you. Be selective in your choices. Choose wisely when adding connections through LinkedIn, which is distinct from Facebook or other social-media choices. Stay in touch with your LinkedIn network colleagues to maintain an active network without an agenda. LinkedIn makes it very easy to stay in touch. I like to think of social media this way: LinkedIn is for business, Facebook for friends, Twitter for purpose, and YouTube for subscribers.

How do I network? When going to a networking event, have a goal to meet one or two people. Get to know them well. Seek new people. Take business cards with you. I am often surprised by how many people say they forgot to bring their cards. Ask them questions. Provide value, not what you want. This is not speed dating. Ask for their business card. Repeat their name. Make a note on the back of the card when and where you met them. Follow up within 24 hours with an email so they remember you. Do not wait to do this. The goal is not to collect business cards; it is to connect. Over time, you will build strong, trusting relationships. Create a win-win relationship. The more often you do this, the more confident you become.

Your network is the golden ticket to career success only if you stay in touch and build strong relationships. Look for opportunities to connect and help people in your network instead of making it all about you. Check in with them periodically to see how they are doing, what they might need, and how you could help. You will feel great when you get to help others in your network. They, one day, might help you or mentor you.

*Inc. Magazine* contained an excellent article on networking called "Eight Things Power Networkers Do to Make Connections" by Minda Zetlin. Check it out at https://www.inc.com/minda-zetlin/8-things-power-networkers-do-make-connections.html

*"One of the most powerful networking practices is to provide immediate value to a new connection. This means the moment you identify a way to help someone you take action."*

– Lewis Howes

## Self-Assessment Questions

| Questions | Responses |
| --- | --- |
| What is the purpose of networking? | |
| How can it help your career? | |
| Do you enjoy networking? | |
| In what areas of networking do you feel you need assistance? | |
| In what areas of networking do you excel? | |
| What was the last networking event you attended? | |
| When and where is the next networking event you will attend? | |
| What value can you create when networking? | |

## Coach/Mentor Questions

| Questions | Responses |
|---|---|
| What networking events have you attended within our company and externally? | |
| Describe how you feel when you go to a networking event. | |
| Do you typically go alone to these events, or do you bring another colleague? | |
| In what areas of networking do you feel you excel? | |
| In what areas of networking do you need help with now? | |
| Is there a networking event you are interested in attending but have not done so yet? | |
| What is stopping you? | |
| How can I support your growth in this area? | |

## O is for Opportunity

Be observant. Look for opportunities to contribute and make a difference. When problems get presented, think through how you can bring value instead of complaining.

One of the best examples of this happened when I started my higher education career as a new culinary faculty member. I had taught at this school for three months before the fall session. The culinary department director told me my class in the fall session started at 7 a.m. So, on the first day of class, I arrived early, set up my class, and by 7:10 a.m., no students were in class. I thought it was strange, so I headed to the Registrar's Office to see the class schedule. The schedule said my class started at 9 a.m., not 7 a.m. I waited in the faculty and staff lounge until class began. Honestly, it was the best two hours I have ever spent. As each new faculty member came into the lounge, they would ask me where to turn in attendance sheets, how to use the copy machine, where the mailboxes were, the class schedule, Registrar's Office, etc. I helped every person even though I was new and did not know everything.

I went to teach my class at 9 a.m. The class ended at noon. I promptly went to the Dean of Education's office and asked to speak with him. I had only met him once, and I was nervous. His assistant said he had time to see me. I explained what had occurred to me that morning: Many new teachers were unsure what to do on the first day of class. I told him that in my previous hospitality industry role, we always held a new employee orientation before anyone started. It helped them feel better connected and more confident in the role. He said, "Great idea. You should do that." I laughed to myself, as they had not given me an orientation, but I said, "Yes, I would be happy to do this." I knew I needed to partner with someone at the school who knew the building, the programs, and all the floors. I found that person in Cliff Willson. I asked him if he would help, and he said yes. So, for the next two years, each quarter, we held the new-employee orientation. Each time we delivered the orientation, it became better and better.

I could have complained about the situation, but I chose a different approach. I believe this situation propelled me into having some of the most amazing career opportunities in higher education over the next seventeen years.

So, think about problems such as processes, plans, or systems you see in your organization that may not be working as well as you think is possible. Reframe problems as opportunities and see where your career takes you.

*"Success is where preparation and opportunity meet."*

– Bobby Unser

## Self-Assessment Questions

| Questions | Responses |
|---|---|
| What problems or gaps have you noticed in the organization that could be viewed as opportunities? | |
| When have you brought solutions to your organization? Provide three examples.<br>    a.<br>    b.<br>    c. | |
| What kind of impact do you want to make? | |
| How will you know you are making progress? | |

## Coach/Mentor Questions

| Questions | Responses |
|---|---|
| Did you learn anything new when you read the example shared as an opportunity? | |
| What problems or gaps have you noticed in the organization that could be viewed as opportunities? | |
| When have you brought solutions to your organization? Provide three examples.<br>a.<br>b.<br>c. | |

| What kind of impact do you want to make? | |
| --- | --- |
| What is one action you can take to improve in this area? | |
| How will you measure your improvement in this area? | |
| How can I support you? | |

## P is for Purpose

One of the big changes during the pandemic was people stopped to think about their purpose and what they wanted in their careers and work environment. A recent McKinsey report (June 3, 2021) found that 70 percent of people define their purpose through work. Millennials, even more so, likely see work as their life's calling (Dhingra, p. 11). The good news is that employees living their purpose at work are six and a half times more likely to have higher resilience. In our own work environment, we find that Generation Z decides on who to work for based on the organization's mission, vision, and values as they look for integration of their purpose and that of the organization.

When you think about your organization and hiring new talent, it is vital to align the organization's purpose to the purpose of the talent you are considering joining your team. Ask them what their purpose is. Once you discover, you can then decide whether it may or may not be a good fit. If your organization does not have a stated purpose, it is time to develop an authentic purpose.

In addition, these two generations are interested in what you are doing in terms of social impact. It is something they consider when accepting a position. It is also important to share with students about purpose and impact.

So, as you consider becoming a leader or you have already taken on a leadership role, what is your purpose? As a teacher, you can affect lives by the number of students you teach each session. When you are an administrator, the numbers change dramatically. It might not be something you have ever considered before. Whatever your accountability is—say, for a department—you potentially affect many lives of students plus the faculty and staff. Thinking in this way, now how would you answer, "What is your purpose?"

There is a well-known story of three bricklayers dating back to 1666. Rodger Dean Duncan updated it in his article "The Why of Work: Purpose and Meaning Really Do Matter" (2018, September 11). There are three bricklayers, all working on the same wall. One bricklayer was asked, "What are you doing?" One bricklayer said, "I am a bricklayer, and I am feeding my family." The second was asked the same question, and he responded, "I am a builder and am building a wall." The third bricklayer, the most productive of the three and future leader of the group, said, "I am a cathedral builder. I am building a great cathedral to the Almighty." What do you think of this parable and how it applies to purpose? Finding a purpose has a lot to do with your attitude and mindset.

*"There is no greater gift to give or receive than to honor your calling. It is why you were born. And how you become most truly alive."*

– Oprah Winfrey

## Self-Assessment Questions

| Questions | Responses |
|---|---|
| What do you value? | |
| What lights you up and makes you feel alive? | |
| What is your purpose as a teacher? What is your *why*? | |
| What is your purpose as a leader? | |
| How can you create a learning-centered work environment where people find meaning and purpose? Be specific. | |
| What did you think of the story of the brick-layers, and how does it apply to purpose and meaning in life? | |
| What are some of the good things you have done to make a difference in the lives of others? | |

**Coach/Mentor Questions**

| Questions | Responses |
|---|---|
| What do you value? | |
| What lights you up and makes you feel alive? | |
| What is your purpose as a teacher? What is your *why*? | |
| What is your purpose as a leader? | |
| How can you create a learning-centered work environment where people find meaning and purpose? Be specific. | |
| What did you think of the story of the brick-layers, and how does it apply to purpose and meaning in life? | |
| What are some of the good things you have done to make a difference in the lives of others? | |
| How can I support you and your purpose? | |

## Q is for Questioning

The art of asking questions seems to dwindle because of the fast pace of business. Taking the time to ask questions will save you time and give you the information you need to make informed decisions. Ask questions such as who, what, when, where, and how. Ask clarifying questions so you understand the message intended. Questions inform, provide answers, and show you have interest. Questions are information disguised as power. The more you ask, the more you learn about people, processes, plans, and passion. The more questions you ask, the more interesting you become. It is not in what you know; it is what you learn. If this is an area of weakness for you, learn how to ask essential questions.

There are specific types of questions for particular situations. As far back as Socrates (470–339 BC), the art of asking and answering questions was used to stimulate critical thinking. It helps inform and educate.

Organizations like the Foundation for Critical Thinking.org have promoted asking questions and providing resources to educators, healthcare practitioners, and the military since the 1980s.

In the education industry, teachers use Bloom's Taxonomy to provide questions to engage in and stimulate discussions. Dr. Benjamin Bloom created the six levels of questioning in 1956: knowledge, comprehension, application, analysis, synthesis, and evaluation. Anderson and Krathwohl, students of Dr. Bloom, updated Bloom's Taxonomy in 2001. They state the updated version in terms of verbs instead of nouns to denote questioning as an action and is not static. They are remember, understand, apply, analyze, evaluate, and create.

Even the Dale Carnegie organization believes that asking questions is an essential people skill. Check out their books and videos online. Questioning helps inform and build connections with others. What questioning models does your organization use?

Reduce your talking, ask more questions, and increase your listening capacity. It might keep you from jumping to the wrong conclusions. If you are not listening, you are filling in the blanks with your thoughts or meaning, which can distort the outcome of the communication.

It might surprise you how attractive you become to others when you are fully present and listening. Think about it. How do you feel when someone really listens to you?

*"The art and science of asking questions is the source of all knowledge."*

– Thomas Berger

## Self-Assessment Questions

| Questions | Responses |
|---|---|
| How is problem-solving related to asking questions? | |
| Have you ever thought about the types of questions you ask? What are they? | |
| Does your organization have a questioning model they use? | |
| Research three questioning resources. It can be online, via books, podcasts, or TED Talks. Be ready to discuss.<br>a.<br><br>b.<br><br>c. | |
| How will you know you are improving your questioning ability? | |

**Coach/Mentor Questions**

| Questions | Responses |
|---|---|
| Problem-solving and asking questions are related. Explain to me the relationship and how it can enhance your promotability traits. | |
| What did you find when you researched three questioning resources? Let us discuss. | |
| How can you help your team members become better at asking questions rather than jumping to conclusions or voicing their opinions? | |
| Compare and contrast two people on your team and their critical thinking abilities. | |
| Create a plan for continuing to develop your critical thinking skills. | |
| How can I support you in questioning? | |

## R is for Resiliency

Greitens (2016), in his incredible book on resilience, describes resilience as the virtue that enables people to move through hardship and improve (p. 3). Examples include veterans who come home with lost limbs or PTSD. Greitens, a former Navy SEAL, understands what being on the frontline means where battles are fought and fates decided, and not everyone understands.

It includes people who have lost loved ones, suffered from a terminal disease, or a friend or family member who committed suicide. It can include a loss of a job, financial loss, health, well-being, etc. It can include losing your freedom.

According to Greitens (2016, p. 5), pain can make or break you. He shares what worked for him and his Navy SEAL brothers and has worked overtime. Questions to focus on are: How do you focus your mind, control your stress, and excel under pressure? How do you work through fear and build courage? How do you overcome defeat and rise above obstacles?

I live by the sayings I have made up to continue to move forward. One that serves me well is, "Circumstances do not define me." When things seem really low, I cannot focus on the moment. I must look forward. I remember to "Let go and let God." You can turn hardship into victory, but it is not easy. You have a choice. Are you going to let the current circumstance defeat you? Remember, God is in control. No one gets through life without a struggle, which is a good thing to remember when going through incredible challenges.

Resilience is the key to having a well-lived life and being able to navigate changes and not resist them. Some of my most painful lessons in life have been the greatest learning and growth opportunities. I did not know it when it was happening, but I can look back and see how far I have come. Stop today and affirm the progress you have made on this journey.

*"Let us not be surprised when we have to face difficulties. When the wind blows hard on a tree, the roots stretch and grow stronger, let it be so with us. Let us not be weaklings yielding to every wind that blows, but strong in the spirit to resist."*

— Amy Carmichael

## Self-Assessment Questions

| Questions | Responses |
|---|---|
| Who are people you admire for their resiliency? | |
| What brings you happiness? | |
| Who are you? | |
| What habits serve you? | |
| How can you become more resilient when learning new technology? | |
| How can you obtain self-mastery? In what areas? | |
| How do you navigate tough times? | |
| What do you need to take responsibility for? | |
| How do you deal with pain and loss? | |
| What are some examples of your resiliency? | |

## Coach/ Mentor Questions

| Questions | Responses |
|---|---|
| Who are people you admire for their resiliency? | |
| What brings you happiness? | |
| Who are you? | |
| What habits serve you? | |
| How can you become more resilient when learning new technology? | |
| How can you obtain self-mastery? In what areas? | |
| How do you navigate tough times? | |
| How do you deal with pain and loss? | |
| What are some examples of your resiliency? | |
| How can I further support you? | |

## S is for Self-Awareness

Self-awareness is the key to your success. If you know yourself, you get it. Have you looked in the mirror lately? How self-aware are you? Do you know where your blind spots are? Can you identify your strengths? Do you know your weaknesses? If you want to improve your self-awareness, here are some approaches.

Based on the last few months of learning and growing, now it is time to stretch yourself. Consider conducting your own personal 360-degree assessment. Find five to seven people who you trust to give you honest feedback but who are not friends who will just tell you what you want to hear. Ask them the following questions: (1) name three of your strength areas; (2) two areas that need to be developed; (3) one thing they find frustrating about you; (4) what they wish for you; (5) what an area of expertise for you is; (6) what your blind spots are; and (7) how you can improve and challenge yourself. Write what they tell you. It will amaze you at what you learn about yourself. Remember, feedback is a gift, so say thank you.

After you did this exercise, what did you learn?

I recently asked a few professional friends what they think their managers think of them. I asked, "How do you think your teachers or managers think you present yourself? How would they describe your personality traits and leadership style? Tone? Nonverbal expressions? Time-management ability? Team player? Problem Solver? Respectful? Contributor? Communication style, personality, etc.?"

They said they did not know. Not knowing is an enormous problem. If you do not know what people around you are thinking, how will you ever be able to improve?

*"Knowing yourself is key to all wisdom."*

– Aristotle, Ancient Greek philosopher

## Self-Assessment Questions

| Questions | Responses |
|---|---|
| What did you learn from the interviews you conducted? | |
| What are three of your strength areas? | |
| What are two areas that need to be developed? | |
| What is one thing they find frustrating about you? | |
| What do they wish for you? | |
| What is an area where you excel? | |
| What are your blind spots? | |
| How can you improve and challenge yourself? | |

## Coach/Mentor Questions

| Questions | Responses |
|---|---|
| Based on the interviews you conducted, what did you learn? | |
| Based on the interviews you conducted, what surprised you? | |
| Have you taken any online self-awareness assessments? If yes, what did you learn or confirm? | |
| Have you ever taken any personal-development courses to discover your blind spots? If so, what classes? What did you find out? | |
| What traits are essential to getting a job or fulfilling your goals? | |
| How can I support you in your quest for self-assessment? | |

## T is for Thank You

When was the last time you said, "Thank you"? Those two words are some of the most powerful for your career and life. When did you last write a handwritten thank-you note? Not an email or a tweet, but a handwritten note. You might think this is old school, but the impression you make by doing this speaks volumes. Taking the time to acknowledge someone means a great deal.

Think about opportunities to say thank you. Did your mentor give you some solid advice? Did you seek a job recommendation, or did someone help you with a letter of recommendation? Did you go out for a job interview and write a follow-up thank you? Were you given a job, and did you say thank you? Were you given a promotion, and did you say thank you? Did you thank your team members when they completed a project on time? Were you given a bonus, and did you say thank you? You might think, *Hey, I earned it. What's the big deal?* That attitude is an entitlement attitude. How about being grateful and saying thank you instead?

Did a coworker take the time to help you out, or did someone remember your birthday or work anniversary? Did someone take you to coffee, lunch, or dinner, and they paid? My husband often takes me out for coffee, knowing I love it. I say thank you every time. I appreciate him and the gesture. I am not saying thank you to get him to do it again. I appreciate it every time. It makes me feel good, and I know he feels appreciated.

Did you attend a company dinner or event and thank the host? Did someone drive you to a meeting, and you said thank you? When was the last time you thanked your boss?

As you can see from the above examples, many opportunities exist to say thank you. If this is not your strong suit, it can be learned. If you schedule reminders on your calendar or put a sticky note by your workstation to do this weekly at a minimum, you will begin the journey of self-mastery. Try it and see what happens! Make this a habit each week.

*"Make it a habit of telling people thank you—to express your appreciation sincerely without expecting anything in return. Truly appreciate those around you, and you will soon find many others around you. Truly appreciate life, and honestly, you will find you have more of it."*

– Ralph Marston

## Self-Assessment Questions

| Questions | Responses |
|---|---|
| Where have you noticed opportunities to say thank you? | |
| Have you noticed missed opportunities to say thank you? | |
| How does it make you feel when you say or write a thank-you note? | |
| Does this come naturally? | |
| Do you need to schedule a reminder on your calendar? | |

## Coach/Mentor Questions

| Questions | Responses |
|---|---|
| There is a statement that is often quoted: "Employees do not quit organizations, they quit supervisors." What does this mean to you? | |
| What kind of employee or leader do you want to be? | |
| How important is it that employees and team members feel appreciated? | |
| What makes you feel appreciated at work? | |
| Where have you noticed opportunities to say thank you? | |
| Have you noticed missed opportunities to say thank you? | |
| How important in business do you think it is to say thank you? | |
| How can I further support you in developing your "thank-you muscle"? | |

## U is for Upskilling

What is the possibility of becoming a role model for our students and staff for upskilling? How can we combine our passion and commitment to making a difference in the world?

Things are changing so quickly; staying current is up to us. Marshall Goldsmith wrote a book titled *What Got You Here Won't Get You There*, which is an appropriate expression of the world and especially for new leaders.

Leadership has identified early on you have something special. It might be the way you connect with people. It might be your subject matter expertise. You will need all of that and so much more. The truth is the first leadership role you take on will be challenging. Some days you'll feel like giving up. This is where your passion, commitment, and resiliency come into play. Reflect on what you want to accomplish and your why. Then determine where you can upskill. Is it business acumen, digital fluency, soft skills, data and research, or something else?

According to McKinsey & Company (2021), reskilling is building a unique skill or set of skills, while upskilling is building a higher level of competency in a skill or skill set to perform better in your role (p.4).

Our role in education is to follow the trends and know how to reskill or upskill. What are the current and future needs? One example is in technology. According to the World Economic Forum, there will be 97 million new jobs by 2025, and we do not have the people with the skills yet to fill these positions (2021, p.1). This will require very specific training. What kind of training will it take to reach young talent to equip them with the practical skills necessary to succeed at work? This may be where you create a program at your institution. McKinsey & Company created a program called Forward and taught 100,00 learners worldwide. They expect the next cohort to include 150,000 learners. Companies on a much smaller scale are creating in-house emerging leaders' programs to address leadership challenges and provide a practical approach to what it takes to succeed and the soft skills necessary.

*"The mark of higher education isn't the knowledge you accumulate in your head. It's the skills you gain about how to learn."*

– Adam Grant

## Self-Assessment Questions

| Questions | Responses |
| --- | --- |
| What is your plan for upskilling opportunities? | |
| What resources do you use to research trends? | |
| Where are the gaps in your organization to help young talent upskill? Staff upskilling? | |
| What solutions can you provide? | |

## Coach/Mentor Questions

| Questions | Responses |
| --- | --- |
| What are your upskilling opportunities? | |
| What resources do you use to research trends? | |
| Where are the gaps in your organization to help young talent upskill? Staff upskilling? | |
| What can you learn now? | |
| How can I support you? | |

## V is for Vision

What vision do you have for your life? Visualize what you want for yourself. What do you love doing? What type of career? What job roles? What salary do you want to earn? What do you want for financial security? What educational level do you want to attain? Where do you want to live? What do you want your relationships to look like? What hobbies do you enjoy? What about spirituality?

Whom do you see yourself becoming? How does it feel? What do you see? Take a mental picture. Write it down. Create a vision board that inspires, motivates, and brings you joy. Place it where you see it every day. There is scientific evidence to support the power of visualization. What you focus on, you achieve.

What are people saying about you? The more you can bring all your senses into this vision you have for yourself, the more likely you will achieve it. Write it down. Look at it every day. Repeat it as an affirmation. Write the goals you want to achieve. Do you believe it is possible? Great, if yes. Get yourself out of the way and make it happen. You are more likely to achieve the life you want if you write down your goals and revisit them daily.

As an emerging leader, it is imperative that you have a vision of where you want to take the organization, department, or team. The more you can paint the picture for them, the more likely you will achieve it. When you are storytelling about the vision, bring in all senses.

One of my former bosses asked us to engage in this great exercise. He would describe the project we were working on, then ask us to close our eyes and think about three years from now. He would say, "Let's pretend we are at a company picnic, celebrating our success. What would we have accomplished? What were people saying about the organization internally and externally? How did you feel? What was the day like? What sounds could you hear? What did you see around you?" By the time we finished the exercise, everyone could see in their mind's eye where we were going and how we would feel when we got there. It is truly inspiring! At subsequent meetings, he would remind us of the picnic picture, so we would not lose sight of where we were going and what we could accomplish.

Good luck!

*"The visionary starts with a clean sheet of paper and reimagines the world."*

– Malcolm Gladwell

## Self-Assessment Questions

| Questions | Responses |
|---|---|
| What do you want for yourself and your life? | |
| What type of career? What job roles? What salary do you want to earn? | |
| What do you want for financial security? | |
| What educational level do you want to attain? | |
| Where do you want to live? | |
| What do you want your relationships to look like? | |
| What hobbies do you enjoy? | |
| What about spirituality? | |
| Whom do you see yourself becoming? How does it feel? What do you see? Write it down. Create a vision board. Create a board that inspires, motivates, and brings you joy. Put it in a place where you'll see it every day. | |

**Coach/Mentor Questions**

| Questions | Responses |
|---|---|
| As an emerging leader, it is imperative that you have a vision of where you want to take the organization, department, or team. How would you describe the picture? | |
| What is the story? | |
| If you were the leader, could you lead the picnic exercise as described? How would you bring in all the senses? Share your version of this exercise with me. | |

## W is for White Lies

I am often surprised at how people tell trivial lies. They feel justified for whatever reason.

Example: "I am going to take home office supplies. It is no big deal. The company can afford it." Would you feel the same way if you owned the company?

Example: "I won't clock out for lunch, and no one will know." Or "I will take an extra ten minutes on my break. Who cares?"

Years ago, I took over a company in desperate financial trouble. I was uncertain for a time whether we would meet payroll every other week. I needed the employees to understand the situation without causing panic. So, I had a little fun with it and asked them to all return our special signature pens the next day. I called it "Amnesty Day." I was looking for a thousand ways to reduce expenses without losing sight of all the details. The next day, we had over a thousand custom signature pens returned. Have I made my point?

It seemed like no big deal for the employees, but it was a symbol for all of us to work together and turn the situation around, and we did. You might feel someone mistreated you, you deserve something, and you justify it. A white lie is a *lie*. *Webster* defines a lie as making an untrue statement intending to deceive. Over time, people forget what the truth is. Lying has a way of holding you hostage. You can justify all you want, but it costs you. It costs you integrity, relationships, jobs, freedom, and authenticity.

A second example is when you tell your supervisor the report is done, but it is not. You built in time to turn it in on time, but you lied to your boss about the present state of the report.

Another example is social media. How truthful do you think you are in how you present yourself on social media? Your photo? Your resume? Your relationships? Your reputation? Is it the truth or a lie?

Other examples include stealing time, not communicating and taking responsibility, and not following a process or company standards. What other examples can you think of?

Be careful: Big Brother is always watching.

*"If you tell the truth, you don't have to remember anything."*

– Mark Twain

## Self-Assessment Questions

| Questions | Responses |
|---|---|
| Where have you told white lies? | |
| How did you justify it? | |
| What did it cost you? Or what could it cost you? | |
| Do you ever think white lies become more significant over time? | |

## Coach/Mentor Questions

| Questions | Responses |
|---|---|
| What did you think about "Amnesty Day" and the returned pens? | |
| Do you think most people feel justified in telling white lies? What do you think the point of it is? | |
| Do you think there is ever a time when a white lie is justified? | |
| How can you create a culture of truth and integrity as a future leader? | |

| How do you model transparency? | |
|---|---|
| How can I support you? | |

## X is for Xper

The definition of xper is to show how much of an expert you are through the behaviors you display, the connections you create, and the results you produce. This can be a way to upskill, build your brand, and become the go-to person.

The workforce outcomes are changing quickly, and there is a real demand for specialists, not generalists. What technical or functional skills are you known for without compromising interpersonal skills? What are the mission-critical competencies of your role? What are the mission-critical competencies for the next role in your company? Become a subject matter expert. Take part in professional associations, attend workshops, earn a certification or an additional degree, read books, listen to podcasts, learn from others around you, and build your network. Enhance your digital literacy. Interested in accelerating your career? Find a mentor or sponsor. Interview a company expert in data management and metrics if this is not an area of expertise.

What interpersonal skills have you fully developed? Emotional intelligence, critical thinking, discipline, humility, change management/innovation, collaboration, conflict resolution, diversity, ethics, or project management? Are there areas in interpersonal skills that could be further developed?

What are your plans for the future? Want to solidify your learning and expertise? Teach others. Form a study group, conduct a lunch and learn, or hold coffee break sessions to help share the learning. Topics could include budgeting, faculty development, hiring the right talent, engagement and retention strategies, event management, etc.

Leadership and learning are a journey.

*"If you want to be successful, it is just that simple. Know what you are doing. Love what you are doing. And believe in what you are doing."*

– Will Rogers, American cowboy, comedian, social commentator, and actor.

## Self-Assessment Questions

| Questions | Responses |
|---|---|
| What functional/technical skills are your areas of expertise? | |
| What are mission-critical competencies for your role? | |
| Are there interpersonal skills that you could further develop? | |
| What are the mission-critical competencies for the next role in your company? | |
| What is an exciting opportunity for you to take on? | |
| What is one area where you excel over the competition? | |
| What will help you focus on continuing to grow in your role? | |
| Do you have a mentor or sponsor? | |
| How will you measure success? | |

## Coach/Mentor Questions

| Questions | Responses |
|---|---|
| What functional/technical skills are your areas of expertise? | |
| What are mission-critical competencies for your role? | |
| What are the mission-critical competencies for the next role in your company? | |
| Are there interpersonal skills that you could further develop? | |
| What will help you focus on continuing to grow in your role? | |
| What is an exciting opportunity for you to take on? | |
| What is one area where you excel over the competition? | |
| Do you have a mentor or sponsor? Explain. | |
| How will you measure success? | |

## Y is for Yearning

Do you have an innate yearning to become a better you? Do you have a zest for life? Do you have a love for learning? Do you yearn to earn? Do you yearn to travel and experience new things? This is not to say you are unsatisfied, but you have energy that encompasses the essence of your being. Yearning is not related to age. Yearning can exist at any age.

Yearning is a strong desire to --

I yearned to teach at the college level, share my professional experiences, and mentor others professionally, which is distinct from coaching. I had academic credentials. I had business experience and a proven track record. But I did not have the tools to deliver an engaging classroom experience at the beginning of my new career path. The yearning was incredible, yet I knew I had to go to work and learn as much as possible to master the art and science of teaching. I attribute that yearning to carry me through those tough times so that I could obtain personal and professional mastery. I genuinely believe all things are possible with yearning, effort, and persistence.

So, explore your possibilities. Explore your values. Explore your beliefs.

What do you yearn for in your life? Be specific and go for it!

*"There are three ingredients for a good life: learning, earning, and yearning."*

– Christopher Morley

## Self-Assessment Questions

| Questions | Responses |
|---|---|
| For what do you yearn? Research areas. | |
| How do you start to make this happen? Create a logical plan. | |
| What could stop you? | |
| What is your timeline? | |
| How will you measure success? | |

## Coach/Mentor Questions

| Questions | Responses |
|---|---|
| For what do you yearn? What areas did you research? | |
| How do you make this happen? What is your plan? | |
| What could stop you? | |

| What is your timeline? | |
| --- | --- |
| How will you measure success? | |
| How can I support you? | |

## Z is for Zone

I have often heard athletes describe being "in the zone" when everything they do seems to go in the right direction. I am sure you have your favorite stories and examples, so you can imagine what being in the zone must feel like.

Being in the zone is described as being in the flow, flow state, or groove. Think back to when you lost track of time because you were in the flow or the zone. Now that we have come to trait Z, number twenty-six, do you feel you are in the zone? Have you ever been in the zone? What does it feel like? What were you doing? Describe the sensations.

How can you get back there if you are not in the zone now? What is your energy level? What goals have you set, or what actions are you taking? Sarah Chang wrote a great article, "The Best Tricks for Getting in the Zone at Work." You can retrieve it at https://www.themuse.com/advice/the-best-tricks-for-getting-in-the-zone-at-work. She describes tools to get back into the flow state. What project can you be working on those challenges you face? What goals do you want to accomplish? Can you create a space with little or few interruptions?

What are you not doing that you need to be doing? What should you keep doing that works or stop doing? Are you committed to returning to being in the zone state and taking it to the next level? Turn off the TV and get started!

*"Everything is energy, and that's all there is to it. Match the frequency of the reality you want, and you can't help but get that reality. It can be no other way. This is not philosophy. This is physics."*

– Albert Einstein

## Self-Assessment Questions

| Questions | Responses |
|---|---|
| Are you in the zone? | |
| Describe when you were in the zone and how it felt. | |
| Do you feel you are in the zone now? | |
| How can you get back in the zone? | |
| Read the research article by Sarah Chang and check out the resources. | |
| Final Reflection: Write what you have accomplished over the last 26 weeks. Be ready to discuss. | |
| What is next? | |

## Coach/Mentor Questions

| Questions | Responses |
| --- | --- |
| Are you in the zone? | |
| After reading the research article by Sarah Chang, what do you think? | |
| How can you help your team get in the zone? | |
| How can I support you? | |
| Final Reflection: Now that you have completed 26 weeks, what do you believe you have accomplished? Use the Self-Awareness Inventory again to evaluate your progress. | |
| What have you learned? | |
| How have you changed? | |
| What is next? | |

**Congratulations on Paving Your Path to From Teacher to Leader. Please take a few minutes to reflect on how far you have come and plan your next steps.**

## Post Assessment Inventory

| ABCs for growth and development | Rate yourself 1–10, with 1 being poor and 10 being excellent | Plan to improve/ resources used |
|---|---|---|
| Attitude | | |
| Brand | | |
| Communication | | |
| Decision-Making | | |
| Energy | | |
| Focus | | |
| Gratitude | | |
| Habits | | |
| Integrity | | |
| Jaded | | |
| Knowledge | | |
| Leadership | | |

| | | |
|---|---|---|
| Mindset | | |
| Networking | | |
| Opportunity | | |
| Purpose | | |
| Questioning | | |
| Resiliency | | |
| Self-Awareness | | |
| Thank You | | |
| Upskilling | | |
| Vision | | |
| White Lies | | |
| Xper | | |
| Yearning | | |
| Zone | | |

# SUMMARY

We collaborated on this book to support our aspiring leaders in education. We wished there had been a book like this when we transitioned into education administration so the path could have been easier.

This book combines self-reflection, advice, and competencies critical to thriving in education administration. Being a leader in education is not for everyone, and we applaud the teachers and faculty members who stay in the classroom and make a difference each day with our students. It is your passion.

For those of you considering being in educational leadership, the path will be enhanced if you have a mentor alongside you. This book is designed to have a weekly accountability partner, your mentor, and a structure to increase your leadership skills. Your mentor could be a supervisor or a peer who you truly admire and can learn from. No one is successful on their own. We wish you a lifetime of career happiness, and hopefully, one day, you will have the opportunity to serve as someone's mentor to guide them along the way.

# REFERENCES

Alton, L. (2016, September 7). *How sleep deprivation affects your day at the office.* https://www.forbes.com/sites/larryalton/2016/09/07/heres-how-sleep-affects-your-day-at-the-office/#3ed1c8e7820b

Anderson. L. & Krathwohl, D. (2001). *Revised Bloom's taxonomy.* https://thesecondprinciple.com/teaching-essentials/beyond-bloom-cognitive-taxonomy-revised/

Anthony, R. (2015). *Self-Assessment Tool- Innovative Leadership.*

Anthony, R. (2016). *Innovative leaders are decisive, driven, action-oriented change agents.*

Ascott, E. (2021, Nov. 19) *AI will create 97 million jobs, but workers don't have the skills required (Yet).* Retrieved on March 14, 2023, from https://allwork.space/2021/11/ai-will-create-97-million-jobs-but-workers-dont-have-the-skills-required-yet/

Aspin, D.N. & Chapman, J.D. (2000). Lifelong learning: concepts and conceptions. International Journal of Lifelong Education, 19(1), 2–19.

Attitude. Retrieved October 24, from https://www.google.com/search?q=attitude+definition&oq=attitude+&aqs=chrome.5.69i57j35i39j0l4.5240j1j8&sourceid=chrome&ie=UTF-8

Beausoleil, M. (2020, March 29). *Ten events that defined a generation: Millennial edition.* Retrieved September 16, 2022, from https://beausoleil.medium.com/ten-events-that-defined-a-generation-millennial-edition-9dd5c2806a32

Beck, R. & Harter, J. (2015). *Managers account for 70% of the variance in employee engagement.* Retrieved August 6, 2022, from http://news.gallup.com/businessjournal/182792/managers-account-variance-employee-engagement.aspx

Bloom, B. (1956). *Bloom's taxonomy.* http://www.nwlink.com/~donclark/hrd/bloom.html

Bradberry, T. & Greaves, J. (2009, June 16). *Emotional Intelligence 2.0.* Amazon LLC.

Brainy Quotes. (n.d.). https://www.brainyquote.com/

Bridges, W. (1980). Transitions: making sense of life's changes. Reading, Mass., Addison Wesley.

Brown, B. (2018, Oct 19). *Dare to Lead: Brave work. Tough conversations. Whole hearts.* Random House, NY.

Bungay, G. (2015, July 13). *Remarkable employees: The characteristics of high potentials.* http://performancecritical.com/remarkable-employees-characteristics-high-potentials/

Buzan, Tony. *Mind mapping.* Retrieved from https://tonybuzan.com/

Carmody. N. J. (2002). *I am thankful.* [Poem]. Retrieved October 1, 2022, from http://www.midnightangel308.com/i_am_thankful_for.htm

Carnegie, D. (2013). *The five essential people skills: How to assert yourself, listen to others, and resolve conflicts.* Retrieved on September 3, 0222 from https://www.youtube.com/watch?v=zvZbeplavY0

Cavoulous, A. (n.d.). *Ways to take on more responsibility at work.* Retrieved on January 5, 2018, from https://www.themuse.com/advice/5-ways-to-take-on-more-responsibility-at-work

Chang, S. (n.d.). *The best tricks for getting in the zone at work.* Retrieved January 5, 2018, from https://www.themuse.com/advice/the-best-tricks-for-getting-in-the-zone-at-work.

Connellan, T. (2002). *Bringing out the best in others!: 3 keys for business leaders, educators, coaches, and parents.* Retrieved on January 5, 2018, from https://www.amazon.com/Bringing-Out-Best-Others-Educators/dp/188516758X/ref=sr_1_1?ie=UTF8&qid=1520700987&sr=8-1&keywords=bringing+out+the+best+in+others

Dale Carnegie. (2018). Retrieved on January 26, 2018, from https://www.dalecarnegie.com/en/franchise-locations

Day, M. (2023). *8 Essential time management strategies.* Retrieved on April 12, 2023, from https://www.liquidplanner.com/blog/8-essential-time-management-strategies/

DeFelice, M. (2019). *What gen z wants at work will blow your mind.* Retrieved on September 16, 2022, from https://www.forbes.com/sites/manondefelice/2019/10/31/what-gen-z-wants-at-work-will-blow-your-mind/?sh=2d23886fb8e7

Dhingra, N. & Schaninger, B. (2021, June 3). *The search for purpose in work.* McKinsey & Company: New York.

Dijulius, J. R. III (2003). *Secret service: Hidden systems that produce unforgettable customer service.* Retrieved on January 5, 2018, from https://www.amazon.com/Secret-Service-Systems-Unforgettable-Customer/dp/0814471714/ref=sr_1_3?ie=UTF8&qid=1520797468&sr=8-3&keywords=secret+service+book

D. L. (Feb. 26, 2019). *Decision Making Processes.* Retrieved from LinkedIn https://www.linkedin.com/pulse/decision-making-processes-david-l-stokes-cce/

*Drucker, P.* (1959). The *landmarks of tomorrow.* New York, NY: Harper Collins Field, J. (2001). Lifelong Education. International Journal of Lifelong Education, 20 (1/2), 3–15.

Duncan, R. D. (2018, Sept. 11). *The why of work: Purpose and meaning really do matter.* Retrieved on March 13, 2023, from https://www.forbes.com/sites/rodgerdeanduncan/2018/09/11/the-why-of-work-purpose-and-meaning-really-do-matter/

Dweck, C. *(2009). Mindset: How we can learn to fulfill our potential.* Retrieved on January 5, 2018, from https://www.amazon.com/Mindset-Psychology-Carol-S-Dweck/dp/0345472322/ref=sr_1_1?ie=UTF8&qid=1518884922&sr=8-1&keywords=mindset+by+carol+dweck

Emmons, R. A. (2004). *The psychology of gratitude.* Retrieved on January 5, 2018, https://www.forbes.com/sites/larryalton/2016/09/07/heres-how-sleep-affects-your-day-at-the-office/#3ed1c8e7820b

Ferrazzi, K. & Raz, T. (2005). *Never eat alone and other secrets to success, one relationship at a time.* Crown Publishing: New York.

Fries, A. (2010, February 9). Sparking creativity in the workplace. *Psychology Today.*

Gordon, J. (2007). *How to deal with energy vampires.* Retrieved on January 5, 2018, http://www.jongordon.com/positive-tip-energy-vampires

Grammarly. (2018). Retrieved on January 5, 2018, from https://www.grammarly.com

Greitens, E. (2016). *Resilience.* New York: First Mariner Books.

Herman, C. (2022, October). *Become a Leader: Developing executive presence.* Coppell, TX.

Hiatt, J. (2006). ADKAR: A model for change in business, government and our community, Learning Center Publications.

Hogan, R. & Hogan, J. (2001). Assessing leadership: a view of the dark side. *International Journal of Evaluation and Assessment*, pp. 9, 40–51.

Holmes, L. (2017, December). *10 things grateful people do differently.* Retrieved on January 5, 2018, from https://www.huffingtonpost.com/entry/habits-of-grateful-people_us_565352a6e4b0d4093a588538

Kaiser, H. (n.d.). *What is problem-solving?* Retrieved on January 5, 2018, https://www.mind-tools.com/pages/article/newTMC_00.htm

Kaye, B.& Jordan-Evans, S. (2008). *Love 'em or lose' em: Getting good people to stay.* Berrett- Koehler Publishers: San Francisco.

Korn Ferry (2014). *FYI-For your improvement:* Competencies development guide.

Kotter, J. P. (1996). Leading Change. Boston: Harvard Business School Press.

Krakoff, S. (2020). *The top 5 conflict resolution strategies for the workplace.* Retrieved on April 12, 2023, from https://online.champlain.edu/blog/top-conflict-resolution-strategies

Lewin K. (1947) Frontiers in group dynamics: Concept, method and reality in social science; equilibrium and social change. Human Relations 1(1): 5–41.

Lewin K. (1951) 'Field Theory in Social Science,' Harper and Row, New York.

Linkner, J. (2011, June 16). 7 steps to a culture of innovation. *Inc.* Retrieved on June 1, 2022, from *https://www.inc.com/articles/201106/josh-linkner-7-steps-to-a-culture-of-innovation.html*

Linkner, J. (2011). *Disciplined dreaming-A proven system to drive breakthrough creativity.* Retrieved on April 16, 2023, from *https://www.amazon.com/Disciplined-Dreaming-Proven-Breakthrough-Creativity/dp/0470922222*

Liotta, A. (2012). *Unlocking generational codes: Understanding what makes the generations tick and what ticks them off.* Retrieved on January 5, 2018, http://resultance.com/

Mathews, M. (2022, January 1). *16 reasons why people stay in their jobs.* Retrieved on September 16, 2022, from https://beststepever.com/16-reasons-why-people-stay-in-their-jobs/

Maxwell, J. C. (2003). *Attitude 101: What every leader needs to know.* Retrieved on January 5, 2018, https://www.amazon.com/Attitude-101-Every-Leader-Needs/dp/0785263500

McKinsey & Co. (2000, May). *Leadership development: Where is the ROI?* Retrieved on September 17, 2022, from www.hri.eckerrd.edu

McKinsey & Co. (2021, Aug. 23). *Piecing together the talent puzzle: When to redeploy, upskill, or reskill.* Retrieved on March 14, 203 from https://www.mckinsey.com/capabilities/people-and-organizational-performance/our-insights/the-organization-blog/piecing-together-the-talent-puzzle-when-to-redeploy-upskill-or-reskill

McKinsey & Co. (2022, August). What is *Leadership?: A definition and way forward.* Retrieved on March 12, 2023, from https://www.mckinsey.com/featured-insights/mckinsey-explainers/what-is-leadership

Moran, G. (2017). *Ditch these seven bad habits before 2018 starts.* Retrieved on January 5, 2018, https://www.fastcompany.com/40503547/ditch-these-seven-bad-habits-before-2018-starts

NA (2018, May 3). *HR advice: Behavioral interviewing yields better results.* Retrieved September 16, 2022, from https://www.bizjournals.com/columbus/news/2018/05/03/hr-advice-behavioral-interviewing-yields-better.html

NA National Speakers Association. (2018). Retrieved on January 5, 2018, https://www.nsa-speaker.org/

Nugent, K. (2017, Nov.). 52 weeks to exceptional leadership: The secret of your success is determined by your ability to lead and inspire your teams. Sojourn Publishing.

Peters, T. (2004). *The brand called you.* Retrieved on January 5, 2018, https://www.fastcompany.com/48979/brand-you-survival-kit

Pfau, B. (2016, April 7). *What do millennials really do at work: The same thing the rest of us do.* Retrieved on September 17, 2022, from https://hbr.org/2016/04/what-do-millennials-really-want-at-work

Porter, M.E. (1996) *What Is Strategy?* Harvard Business Review, 74, 61–78.

Pulver, C. (2021). *I love it here: How great leaders create organizations their people never want to leave.* Canada: Raincoast Books.

Reynolds, J. (2017, March 1). *20 characteristics of high-potential employees.* Retrieved on January 5, 2018, from https://www.tinypulse.com/blog/20-characteristics-of-high-potential-employees

Rippy, R. (2017). *Love revolution: A 21-day program to create a life you love.* Retrieved on January 5, 2018, from https://www.facebook.com/events/880164042160109/

Schmidt, C. (2022). *The power of agile recruiting.* Lever. Retrieved on September 17, 2022, from https://www.lever.co/resources/ebook/the-power-of-agile-recruiting/

Sinek, S. (2011). *Start with why: How great leaders inspire action.* Retrieved on January 5, 2018, https://www.ted.com/talks/simon_sinek_how_great_leaders_inspire_action

Smith, Bedford, G. (October 28). *5 ways to promote creativity in the workplace.* Retrieved on April 16, 2023, from https://www.bizjournals.com/bizjournals/feature/small-business/tip-of-the-month-creativity.html

Straker, David (1997). *Rapid Problem Solving with Post-it Notes. The Business Journals.*

TED Talks. (2018). Retrieved on January 5, 2018, from https://www.youtube.com/channel/UCAuUUnT6oDeKwE6v1NGQxug

The Foundation for Critical Thinking. (2018). Retrieved on January 5, 2018, from https://www.criticalthinking.org/

Toastmasters International (2018). Retrieved on January 5, 2018, from https://www.toastmasters.org/

Tree, C. (2017). Why They Buy: Cracking the Personality Code to Achieve Record Sales and Real Wealth. Aviva Publishing.

Warhawk, M. S. (2007, December 27). *No excuses.* [Video]. YouTube. https://www.youtube.com/watch?v=obdd31Q9PqA

Yaffe, P. (2011, October). *7% rule fact, fiction or misunderstanding.* DOI: 10.1145/2043155.20453156.

# ABOUT THE AUTHORS

## Dr. Eric Goodman

Dr. Eric Goodman brings his expertise in higher education to his work in helping schools rethink, reimagine, and reinvent their futures. As a sought-after speaker, Eric is President of Higher Ed Change, an educational improvement firm guiding institutions through a process of transformation that creates a highly productive culture and organization and ultimately maximizes student success. He also serves as a coach, consultant, and trainer for educators, business leaders, and individuals who look to overcome challenges, plan for the future, and maximize success. His reason for being is rooted in serving as a catalyst for positive growth and transformation in the lives he touches, including thousands of educators.

Dr. Goodman has over 25 years of broad experience as a results-oriented and data-driven leader in consulting, corporate, and higher education settings. As a visionary innovator with a proven track record of success related to strategic planning and leading organizational development and change, he has also published articles and book chapters in areas related to organizational culture, change management, and teamwork.

He has served as a professor and leader in higher education with over a decade in the C-Suite and another decade as a business school dean, including leading one of the nation's largest College of Business with over 22,000 students. His extensive leadership and consulting work has allowed him to test the strategies in this book in the real world of educators and their rapidly changing environment.

Dr. Goodman holds a Ph.D. in Business Administration with a focus in Organization Development from the University of Colorado at Boulder, where he also earned a master's degree in business administration and a bachelor's degree in marketing.

## Dr. Kim Nugent

Dr. Kim Nugent is an innovation leadership coach, MCC SCC coach, keynote speaker, best-selling author, and the founder of Kim Nugent Enterprises LLC. She was recently selected for the prestigious Lifetime Achievement Award for 2022 by IAOTP and chosen to be featured in the "Top 50 Fearless Leaders" publication by the International Association of Top Professionals (IAOTP).

Dr. Nugent's areas of expertise include but are not limited to improving operational effectiveness, creating mentorship programs, professional development, student success, improving retention rates, motivational speaking, innovation leadership training, private career and leadership coaching, higher education faculty development, and executive leadership development. She has thirty years of knowledge and experience.

In addition to her successful career, Kim is a sought-after lecturer, speaker, and best-selling Amazon award-winning author. To date, Dr. Nugent has written and published six books (this being her seventh):

*Did I Say Never?*
*52 Weeks to Exceptional Leadership*
*Promotion Protocol: Unlock the Secrets to Promotability and Career Success*
*Coaching Conversations* (workbook to support *Promotion Protocol*)
*Paving Your Path: What's Next for High School Graduates*
*From Prison to Possibilities*

# CONNECT WITH OTHER RESOURCES

If you found the information and developmental approach of this book helpful, we invite you to unlock the path to educational leadership by visiting and sharing this website with other educators: www.teachertoleader.com

***Scan Me***

In addition, since you've finished this book if you'd like to **claim a wealth of powerful resources** including complimentary downloads specifically designed to empower teachers to step into impactful roles as leaders please visit www.teachertoleader.com/resources today and embark on a transformative journey towards becoming an influential leader in the field of education.

***Scan Me***

Our website offers invaluable resources to enhance your skills, foster growth, and unleash your leadership potential. Don't miss this opportunity to take your education career to new heights.

*We invite you to leave a review of this*
*book on Amazon and Goodreads*

# THANK YOU AND OUR COMMITMENT TO YOUR JOURNEY

We are grateful that you chose to read our book. It is an honor to have you join us on this journey. We encourage you to pursue your goals and dreams, and to never give up on your passion. Remember, that leadership is an ongoing process and we are here to support and guide you along the way.

If you would like additional support, we invite you to reach out to us through www.teachertoleader.com or by contacting us to explore how our coaching, consulting, speaking and training services will support you and your organization.

Higher Ed Change, Dr. Eric Goodman, Eric@higheredchange.com or Eric@drericgoodman.com (leadership, faculty and staff development, executive and professional coaching, retention, growth strategies, online learning, academic and student services, curriculum development, competency based education, quality enhancement and accreditation services).

Kim Nugent Enterprises, Dr. Kim Nugent, Nugent1234@gmail.com or kim@ drnugentspeaks.com (faculty development, leadership development, and coaching services provided to increase engagement and retention).